D1210296

FOAL

Also by John Ashbery

HOTEL LAUTRÉAMONT

HOTEL
LAUTRÉAMONT

JOHN ASHBERY

ALFRED A. KNOPF NEW YORK 1992

CENTRAL LIBRARY
1015 North Quincy Street
Arlington, Virginia 22201

This is a Borzoi Book published by Alfred A. Knopf, Inc.

Copyright © 1992 by John Ashbery

All rights reserved under international and Pan-American Copyright Conventions. Published in the United States by Alfred A. Knopf, Inc., New York, and simultaneously in Canada by Random House of Canada Limited, Toronto. Distributed by Random House, Inc., New York.

Owing to limitations of space, all acknowledgments of permission to reprint previously published material will be found at the end of the book.

Library of Congress Cataloging-in-Publication Data
Ashbery, John.
Hotel Lautréamont / John Ashbery. — 1st ed.
p.   cm.
ISBN 0-679-41512-2
I. Title.
PS3501.S475H59   1992
811'.54—dc20   92-52952   CIP

Manufactured in the United States of America
First Edition

FOR PIERRE

CONTENTS

HOTEL LAUTRÉAMONT

LIGHT TURNOUTS

Dear ghost, what shelter
in the noonday crowd? I'm going to write
an hour, then read
what someone else has written.

You've no mansion for this to happen in.
But your adventures are like safe houses,
your knowing where to stop an adventure
of another order, like seizing the weather.

We too are embroiled in this scene of happening,
and when we speak the same phrase together:
"We used to have one of those,"
it matters like a shot in the dark.

One of us stays behind.
One of us advances on the bridge
as on a carpet. Life—it's marvelous—
follows and falls behind.

AND FORGETTING

When I last saw you, in a hurry to get back and stuff,
we wore tape measures and the kids could go to the movies.

I loomed in that background. The old man looked strangely at the sea.
Always feet come knocking at the door
and when it isn't that, it's something or other
melancholy. There is always someone who will find you disgusting.
I love to tear you away from most interests
with besotted relish, and we
talked to each other. Worked before, it'll
work this time.

Look for the strange number at number seven. You see
I need a reason to go down to the sea in ships
again. How does one do that? The old man
came back from looking at it his replies were facile.
Rubber snake or not, my most valued fuchsia
sputtered in the aquarium, at once all shoulders
began to support me. We were travelling in an inn.
You were going to make what design an apple?

Then the hotel people liked us so,
it could have been before a storm, I lie back
and let the wind come to me, and it does, something
I wouldn't have thought of. We can take our meals
beside the lake balustrade. Something either does or
will not win the evidence hidden in this case.
The plovers are all over—make that "lovers," after all
they got their degrees in law and medicine, no one will persist
in chasing them in back lots, the sanded way
I came through here once.

These days the old man often coincides with me; his remarks
have something playful and witty about them, though they do not
hold together. And I, I too have something to keep from him:
something no one must know about.

I'm sure they'll think we're ready now.
We aren't, you know. An icebox grew there once.
Hand me the chatter and I'll fill the plates with cookies,
for they can, they must, be passed.

THE LARGE STUDIO

It's one thing to get them to admit it,
quite another to get soap in your eye.
As long as I can remember I have been cared for,
stricken, like that. No one seems to scold.

I have had so many identity crises
in the last fifty years you wouldn't believe it.
Suffice it to say I am well,
if you like peacock's feathers on pianos
and cars racing their motors,
waiting for dates who never get done with doing their hair.
There have been so many velocipedes, millipedes,
and other words that I'm token senseless.
Just bring me one more drop of the elixir:
that's all I ask.

But when you saw how many colors things come in
it was going to be a long rest of the day.
"Enjoy your afternoon," he said, and it was roses
that you never get enough of and they make you sick.

It was kind of a cable
from which depended seven-branched candelabra
and feathers on the pine trunks
in that witch wood where nobody was supposed to stay—
say, do you think I could? Smell the roses?
Live like it was time?

Lo, it is time.
He raised the horn to his lips.
Such an abundance of—do you mind if I stay,
stay overnight? For the plot of a morrow
is needed to sort out the pegs in, meanwhile enough of me

lasts to give us the old semblance of a staring, naked truth,
with drinks, that we wanted, right?
And because a gray dustman slips by
unnoticed, a thousand cathartic things begin to happen.
Only we know nothing of these. Nothing can take their place.

Today I squeezed a few more drops of color
hoping to blot you out, your face I mean, and then this
extraordinarily tall caller asked if this was something I usually did.
Do I work against the plait often?
And sure, his boots were the right size. I replaced
my little brush and with it the thought of your coming
to absent me after dust and bougainvillea had chimed.
The answer was a nut.

And then there are so many harridans all over
the wall one is encouraged not toward a strict accounting
of all that is taking place, and we have washed, we are nice
for now. And the bowsprit (a word
I have never understood) comes undone, comes all over me, washes
my pure identity from me—help! In the meantime your friend has tunnelled
even as far as us, and it gets to be cold and damp
because the days are no longer making sense, are coming unlocked
in the tin aviary where we pinned them, and no one

right now has any good to say about what temperature
clashes with what other kind statistic we were all against
when it came out but who remembers that now?
Who was even engaged when we first thought of that?

I'll bite your toes, see you in the morning.
Place the canopy on that old chest
allowing for a few grunts and drizzles, please,
and not another word of what you spoke to your father.

THE GARDEN OF FALSE CIVILITY

Where are you? Where you are is the one thing I love,
yet it always escapes me, like the lilacs in their leaves,
too busy for just one answer, one rejoinder.
The last time I see you is the first
commencing of our time to be together, as the light of the days
remains the same even as they grow shorter,
stepping into the harness of winter.

Between watching the paint dry and the grass grow
I have nothing too tragic in tow.
I have this melting elixir for you, front row
tickets for the concert to which all go.
I ought to
chasten my style, burnish my skin, to get that glow
that is all-important, so that some
may hear what I am saying as others disappear
in the confusion of unintelligible recorded announcements.
A great many things were taking place that day,

besides, it was not the taxpayers
who came up to me, who were important,
but other guests of the hotel
some might describe as dog-eared,
apoplectic. Measly is a good word to describe
the running between the incoming and the outgoing tide
as who in what narrow channels shall ever
afterwards remember the keen sightings of those times,
the reward and the pleasure.
Soon it was sliding out to sea
most naturally, as the place to be.

They never cared, nor came round again.
But in the tent in the big loss
it was all right too. Besides, we're not
serious, I should have added.

AUTUMN TELEGRAM

Seen on a bench this morning: a man in a gray coat
and apple-green tie. He couldn't have been over fifty,
his mild eyes said, and yet there was something of the ruthlessness
of extreme old age about his bearing; I don't know what.
In the corner a policeman; next, sheaves of wheat
laid carefully like dolls on the denuded sward,
prompting me to wish of dreaming you again. After the station
we never made significant contact again. But it's all right,
isn't it, I mean the telling had to be it. There was such fire
in the way you put your finger against your nostril
as in some buried sagas erupts out at one sometimes: the power
that is under the earth, no I mean in it. And if all the
disappointed tourists hadn't got up and gone away, we would still
be in each other's reserve, aching, and that would be the same,
wouldn't it, as far as the illustrations and the index were concerned?

As it is I frequently get off before the stop that is mine
not out of modesty but a failure to keep the lines of communication
open within myself. And then, unexpectedly, I am shown a dog
and asked to summarize its position in a few short, angular adverbs
and tell them this is what they do, why we can't count
on anything unexpected. The waterfall is all around us,
we have been living in it, yet to find the hush material
is just what these daily exercises force on us. I mean
the scansions of tree to tree, of house to house, and how
almost every other one had something bright to add
to the morass of conversation: not much, just a raised eyebrow
or skirt. And we all take it in, even laughing in the right places,
which get to be few and far between. Still it is a way of saying,
a meaning that something has been done, a thing, and hearing always
comes afterward. And once you have heard, you know,
the margin can excuse you. We all go back to being attentive
then, and the right signals concur. It stops, and smarts.

NOTES FROM THE AIR

A yak is a prehistoric cabbage: of that, at least, we may be sure.
But tell us, sages of the solarium, why is that light
still hidden back there, among house-plants and rubber sponges?
For surely the blessed moment arrived at midday

and now in mid-afternoon, lamps are lit,
for it is late in the season. And as it struggles now
and is ground down into day, complaints
are voiced at the edges of darkness: look, it says,

it has to be this way and no other. Time that one seizes
and takes along with one is running through the holes
like sand from a bag. And these sandy moments
accuse us, are just what our enemy ordered,

the surly one on his throne of impacted
gold. No matter if our tale be interesting
or not, whether children stop to listen and through the rent
veil of the air the immortal whistle is heard,

and screeches, songs not meant to be listened to.
It was some stranger's casual words, overheard in the wind-blown
street above the roar of the traffic and then swept
to the distant orbit where words hover: *alone,* it says,

but you slept. And now everything is being redeemed,
even the square of barren grass that adjoins your doorstep,
too near for you to see. But others, children and others, will
when the right time comes. Meanwhile we mingle, and not

because we have to, because some host or hostess
has suggested it, beyond the limits of polite

conversation. And we, they too, were conscious of having
known it, written on the flyleaf of a book presented as a gift

at Christmas 1882. No more trivia, please, but music
in all the spheres leading up to where the master
wants to talk to you, place his mouth over yours,
withdraw that human fishhook from the crystalline flesh

where it was melting, give you back your clothes, penknife,
twine. And where shall we go when we leave? What tree is bigger
than night that surrounds us, is full of more things,
fewer paths for the eye and fingers of frost for the mind,

fruits halved for our despairing instruction, winds
to suck us up? If only the boiler hadn't exploded one
could summon them, icicles out of the rain, chairs enough
for everyone to be seated in time for the lesson to begin.

STILL LIFE WITH STRANGER

Come on, Ulrich, the great octagon
of the sky is passing over us.
Soon the world will have moved on.
Your love affair, what is it
but a tempest in a teapot?

But such storms exude strange
resonance: the power of the Almighty
reduced to its infinitesimal root
hangs like the chant of bees,
the milky drooping leaves of the birch
on a windless autumn day—

Call these phenomena or pinpoints,
remote as the glittering trash of heaven,
yet the monstrous frame remains,
filling up with regret, with straw,
or on another level with the quick grace
of the singing, falling snow.

You are good at persuading
them to sing with you.
Above you, horses graze forgetting
daylight inside the barn.

Creeper dangles against rock-face.
Pointed roofs bear witness.
The whole cast of characters is imaginary
now, but up ahead, in shadow, the past waits.

HOTEL LAUTRÉAMONT

1 /
Research has shown that ballads were produced by all of society
working as a team. They didn't just happen. There was no guesswork.
The people, then, knew what they wanted and how to get it.
We see the results in works as diverse as "Windsor Forest" and "The Wife of
    Usher's Well."

Working as a team, they didn't just happen. There was no guesswork.
The horns of elfland swing past, and in a few seconds
We see the results in works as diverse as "Windsor Forest" and "The Wife of
    Usher's Well,"
or, on a more modern note, in the finale of the Sibelius violin concerto.

The horns of elfland swing past, and in a few seconds
The world, as we know it, sinks into dementia, proving narrative passé,
or in the finale of the Sibelius violin concerto.
Not to worry, many hands are making work light again.

The world, as we know it, sinks into dementia, proving narrative passé.
In any case the ruling was long overdue.
Not to worry, many hands are making work light again,
so we stay indoors. The quest was only another adventure.

2 /
In any case, the ruling was long overdue.
The people are beside themselves with rapture
so we stay indoors. The quest was only another adventure
and the solution problematic, at any rate far off in the future.

The people are beside themselves with rapture
yet no one thinks to question the source of so much collective euphoria,
and the solution: problematic, at any rate far off in the future.
The saxophone wails, the martini glass is drained.

Yet no one thinks to question the source of so much collective euphoria.
In troubled times one looked to the shaman or priest for comfort and counsel.
The saxophone wails, the martini glass is drained,
And night like black swansdown settles on the city.

In troubled times one looked to the shaman or priest for comfort and counsel
Now, only the willing are fated to receive death as a reward,
and night like black swansdown settles on the city.
If we tried to leave, would being naked help us?

3 /
Now, only the willing are fated to receive death as a reward.
Children twist hula-hoops, imagining a door to the outside.
If we tried to leave, would being naked help us?
And what of older, lighter concerns? What of the river?

Children twist hula-hoops, imagining a door to the outside,
when all we think of is how much we can carry with us.
And what of older, lighter concerns? What of the river?
All the behemoths have filed through the maze of time.

When all we think of is how much we can carry with us
Small wonder that those at home sit, nervous, by the unlit grate.
All the behemoths have filed through the maze of time.
It remains for us to come to terms with *our* commonalty.

Small wonder that those at home sit nervous by the unlit grate.
It was their choice, after all, that spurred us to feats of the imagination.
It remains for us to come to terms with our commonalty
And in so doing deprive time of further hostages.

4 /
It was their choice, after all, that spurred us to feats of the imagination.
Now, silently as one mounts a stair we emerge into the open
and in so doing deprive time of further hostages,
to end the standoff that history long ago began.

Now, silently as one mounts a stair we emerge into the open
but it is shrouded, veiled: we must have made some ghastly error.
To end the standoff that history long ago began
Must we thrust ever onward, into perversity?

But it is shrouded, veiled: we must have made some ghastly error.
You mop your forehead with a rose, recommending its thorns.
Must we thrust ever onward, into perversity?
Only night knows for sure; the secret is safe with her.

You mop your forehead with a rose, recommending its thorns.
Research has shown that ballads were produced by all of society;
Only night knows for sure. The secret is safe with her:
the people, then, knew what they wanted and how to get it.

ON THE EMPRESS'S MIND

Let's make a bureaucracy.
First, we can have long lists of old things,
and new things repackaged as old ones.
We can have turrets, a guiding wall.
Soon the whole country will come to look over it.

Let us, by all means, have things in night light:
partly visible. The rudeness that poetry often brings
after decades of silence will help. Many
will be called to account. This means that laundries
in their age-old way will go on foundering. Is it any help
that motorbikes whiz up, to ask for directions
or colored jewelry, so that one can go about one's visit
a tad less troubled than before, lightly composed?

No one knows what it's about anymore.
Even in the beginning one had grave misgivings
but the enthusiasm of departure swept them away
in the green molestation of spring.
We were given false information on which
our lives were built, a pier
extending far out into a swollen river.
Now, even these straws are gone.

Tonight the party will be better than ever.
So many mystery guests. And the rain that sifts
through sobbing trees, that excited skiff . . .
Others have come and gone and wrought no damage.
Others have caught, or caused darkness, a long vent
in the original catastrophe no one has seen.
They have argued. Tonight will be different. Is it better for you?

THE PHANTOM AGENTS

We need more data re our example, earth—how it would behave in a
crisis, under pressure,
or simply on a day no one had staked out for unrest
to erupt. What season would fit its lifestyle
most naturally? Who would the observers, the control group be?

For this we must seek the answer in decrepit cinemas
whose balconies were walled off decades ago: on the screen
(where, in posh suburbia, a woman waits),
under the seats, in the fuzz and ancient vomit and gumwrappers;
or in the lobby, where yellowing lobby cards announce
the advent of next week's Republic serial: names
of a certain importance once, names that float
in the past, like a drift of gnats on a summer evening.

Who in the world despises our work
as much as we do? I was against campaigning again,
then my phone started ringing off the hook. I tell you . . .
But to come back to us, sanded down to the finer grain
and beyond—this is what books teach you, but also
what we must do. Make a name, somehow,
in the wall of clouds behind the credits, like a
twenty-one-vehicle pileup on a fog-enclosed highway.
This is what it means to be off and running, off
one's nut as well. But in a few more years,
with time off for good behavior . . .

FROM ESTUARIES, FROM CASINOS

It's almost two years now.
The theme was articulated, the brightness filled in.
And when we tell about it
no wave of recollection comes gushing back—
it's as though the war had never happened.
There's a smooth slightly concave space there instead:
not the ghost of a navel. There are pointless rounds to be made.

No one who saw you at work would ever believe that.
The memories you ground down, the smashed perfection:
Look, it's wilted, but the shape of a beautiful table remains.
There are other stories, too ambiguous even for our purposes,
but that's no matter. We'll use them and someday,
a name-day,
a great event will go unreported.

All that distance, you ask, to the sun?
Surely no one is going to remember to climb
where it insists, poking about
in an abstract of everyday phrases? People have better
things to do with their lives than count how many
bets have been lost, and we all know the birds were here once.
Here they totter and subside, even in surviving.

In history, the best bird catchers were brought before the king,
and he did something, though nobody knows when.
That was before you could have it all
by just turning on the tap, letting it run
in a fiery stream from house to garage—
and we sat back, content to let the letter of the thing notice us,
untroubled by the spirit, talking of the next gull to fly away
on the cement horizon, not quibbling, unspoken for.

We should all get back to the night that bore us
but since that is impossible a dream may be the only way:
dreams of school, of travel, continue to teach and unteach us
as always the heart flies a little away,
perhaps accompanying, perhaps not. Perhaps a familiar spirit,
possibly a stranger, a small enemy whose boiling point
hasn't yet been reached, and in that time
will our desire be fleshed out, at any rate
made clearer as the time comes
to examine it and draw the rasping conclusions?

And though I feel like a fish out of water I
recognize the workmen who proceed before me,
nailing the thing down.
Who asks anything of me?
I am available, my heart pinned in a trance
to the notice board, the stone
inside me ready to speak, if that is all that can save us.

And I think one way or perhaps two; it doesn't matter
as long as one can slip by, and easily
into the questioning but not miasmal dark.
Look, here is a stance—
shall you cover it, cape it? I
don't care he said, going down all those stairs
makes a boy of you. And I had what I want
only now I don't want it, not having it, and yet it defers
to some, is meat and peace and a wooden footbridge
ringing the town, drawing all in after it. And explaining the way to go.

After all this I think I
feel pretty euphoric. Bells chimed, the sky healed.
The great road unrolled its vast burden,
the climate came to the rescue—it always does—

and we were shaken as in a hat and distributed on the ground.
I wish I could tell the next thing. But in dreams I can't,
so will let this thing stand in for it, this me
I have become, this loving you either way.

COP AND SWEATER

It's about this undulation thing,
how we were all beginners to get in on it when it began.
Once that had happened, there was another face on things:
trees no longer came to the door; the seasons
were always "forgetting" to include you in the list—
that sort of thing.

Now those homeless hirsutes we call men
are on our backs, there is no breath out of the kingdom.
Sometimes a plan will come
to take one of them away
but there are long pauses in which grass grows tall
above the elementary wall
behind which bricks, adders and valuable prizes are combined.
It is that we have no mind:
each of us has sampled so many of the others',
and now the concert is sick.
No rain to stay away from any more,
only a darkling yew
that lets pass a few
into the waiting cemetery
to mingle with the military
whose buttons are celebratory.

A man could smash through this, drain the Slough of Despond,
build individual habitats for bird and person,
suitable, and folly too.

I believe it already happened
in some oasis of desert sand
where they are only waiting to know now
what went on back here, so as to leave
and plant other destinies in the star-filled track

the moon makes on water. Then release
happiness to the wineries and rain barrels
where so much could have happened, and does,
even today! Peace to the fawns,
the tied-back curtains. This is the living,
and if we are to be more than music, the waving
shawls and fanlights of a greater possibility
than mine, than us. So we see always.
From the universal boutique each of us stumbles on.

MUSICA RESERVATA

Then I reached the field and I thought
this is not a joke not a book
but a poem about something—but what? Poems are such odd little jiggers.
This one scratches himself, gets up, then goes off to pee
in a corner of the room. Later looking quite
stylish in white jodhpurs against the winter
snow, and in his reluctance to talk to the utterly
discursive: "I will belove less than feared . . ."

He trotted up, he trotted down, he trotted all around the town.
Were his relatives jealous of him?
Still the tock-tock machinery lies half-embedded in sand.
Someone comes to the window, the wave is a gesture proving nothing,
and that nothing has receded. One gets caught
in servants like these and must lose the green leaves,
one by one, as an orchard is pilfered, and then, with luck,
nuggets do shine, the baited trap slides open.
We are here with our welfare intact.

Oh but another time, on the resistant edge of night
one thinks of the pranks things are.
What led the road that sped underfoot
to oases of disaster, or at least the unknown?
We are born, buried for a while, then spring up just as
everything is closing. Our desires are extremely simple:
a glass of purple milk, for example, or a dream
of being in a restaurant. Waiters encourage us, and squirrels.
There's no telling how much of us will get used.

My friend devises the cabbage horoscope
that points daily to sufficiency. He and all those others go home.
The walls of this room are like Mykonos, and sure enough,
green plumes toss in the breeze outside

that underscores the stillness of this place
we never quite have, or want. Yet it's wonderful, this
being; to point to a tree and say don't I know you from somewhere?
Sure, now I remember, it was in some landscape somewhere,
and we can all take off our hats.

At night when it's too cold
what does the rodent say to the glass shard?
What are any of us doing up? Oh but there's
a party, but it too was a dream. A group of boys
was singing my poetry, the music was an anonymous
fifteenth-century Burgundian anthem, it went something like this:

"This is not what you should hear,
but we are awake, and days
with donkey ears and packs negotiate
the narrow canyon trail that is
as white and silent as a dream,
that is, something *you* dreamed.
And resources slip away, or are pinned
under a ladder too heavy to lift.
Which is why you are here, but the mnemonics
of the ride are stirring."

That, at least, is my hope.

SUSAN

Flotsam, I told you, isn't the same as jetsam.
The latter is "cast overboard by the master,
to lighten the load in time of distress."
And as for lagan, it's very different, it's
"debris washed up from the sea, the right to possess such debris,"
or "goods thrown into the sea with a buoy attached
in order that they may be found again."

See what I mean? It's folk art,
as the shy scrolls around the oarlocks announce:
free booty. For everybody. For everybody on that wet strand,
anyway. Waves race to deliver the goods.
I want to get one of those big bags of music
before it's too late, before the sale ends
and we're left without even a fashion
to stand tiptoe on. Though that's when I'll find out
at last what my profession is,
staunch the energy hemorrhaging from my career,
and get back to work again. You know something?

You have the name of a street, that holds
wiles, incantations, thread, in memory of
the mess that made us. You're indigent
as an apple. There is nothing of substance here:
pink sky, gray buildings, white flowers,
a cup that lacks a base . . .

Are they annuals or perennials?
What does it mean to be a bush that grows
some of the year and then rests
until we decide to celebrate it
into trope? She said how quickly that poet followed too,
and after that the peninsula was stilled.

THE KING

So have I heard and do in part believe it.
                                        —*Hamlet*

I /

And you forgave the bastards
for a time
and even so their revenge amazes you.
Alarms wilt in our noon, the winding
roads mark the changing grades of the hills,
hovel and monastery fall.

At last night approached:
"Use me as you will, my properties
are yours; hallow or besmirch them."
How come no god sees
the tears that ooze from under
rusty eyelids? The road is
pitted and incorrect but it happens
to lie in territory that is ours.
We shall chase
the heavenly
bandit:

handlebars
of snow anchor the tole
steeple, so much
that is not ours, and the tale
besides, of bedouins
who broke out of silence as a river
assaults a dam.
                    These, our cold
possessions. The gods are never quite forgotten.

2 /

In June the plaited sheaves are still
undreamt of; the highest
prophecy is only a moment gathering
in a sibyl's throat like a tuck in a shirt.
In that moment, live some of
winter's peace. We can be seen
wearing our oldest clothes when it
shifts abruptly to darkness's excitement:
falling down with bears and our tears
cleanse the past, stiff architecture
too tired to mope, the actual thing,
hinge the story wrests from sleep,
lit in daybreak. And fools and
sages can read this, and it concerns them all.

But there where
the bend in the river is unseen,
watch out! And over all the
slopes we used to think of as our own
millennial rails have pierced
to the aquifers. No explanation
is offered, and none necessary.

THE WHOLE IS ADMIRABLY COMPOSED

In rainy night all the faces look like telephones.
Help me! I am in this street because I was
going someplace, and now, not to be there is here.
So billows pile up on the shore, I hear
the mountains, the tide of autumn pulls in
ever thicker like a blanket of tears, and

people go about their business, unconcerned
if with another. And to those whose loneliness
shouts envy in my face, I say I am here on this
last floor, room of sobs and of grieving.
It's better you know to actually live it
since always some unexpected detail intervenes:
how he came to your house long ago
on a forgotten afternoon filled with birds' wings
and the standard that stood then has crumpled
yet another has taken its place:

high up in the ivy where the water from the
falls disappears amid smooth boulders,
this renown, this envy. And most of all
the challenge sleep brings, how it coaxes
the dunce out of his lair, how meals are shared
and whispers passed around. Then the real boy
comes to you like a kite on wind that is flagging
through the needle hole of the hourglass—
as though this were the summit.

There is more to inconstancy than you will
want to hear, and meanwhile the streets have dried,
tears been put away until another time, and a smile
paints the easy vapor that rises from all
human activity. I see it is time to question trees,

thorns in hedges, again, the same blind investigation
that leads you from trap to trap before bargaining
to forget you. And this is only a bump
on the earth's surface, casting no shadow, until
the white and dark fruits of the far pledge be
wafted into view again, out of control, shimmering
in the dark that runs off and is collected
in oceans. And the map is again wiped clean.

BY FORCED MARCHES

the prodigal returns—to what mechanical
consternation, din of slaughtered cattle.
It was better in the wilderness—there at least
the mind wanders daintily as a stream meanders
through a meadow, for no apparent reason.
And one can catch snatches of the old cries
that were good before this place began
on a day some seventeen centuries ago.

We have reached the tip of a long breakwater
dividing the lake from the deeper and silenter ship channel.
A still-functioning beacon flashes there, proud
of its purpose and its reflection in the night.
There is nothing to do except observe the horizon,
the only one, that seems to want to sever itself
from the passing sky.

Now the links we had left behind
must be reassembled, since this is the land we came from.
It is no place for the squeamish. But as a finger triggers
a catapult, so is the task of the day discharged.

There were many of us at the stream's tip.
I squatted nearby trying to eavesdrop on the sailors'
conversations, to learn where they were going. Finally
one comes to me and says I can have the job if I want it.
Want it! and so in this prismatic whirlpool I am renewed
for a space of time that means nothing to me.

And there is dancing under the porches—so be it.
I am all I have. I am afraid. I am left alone.

Yet it is the way to a certain kind of satisfaction.
I kiss myself in the mirror. And children are kind,
the boardwalk serves as a colorful backdrop
to the caprices acted out, the pavanes and chaconnes
that greet the ear in fragments, melodious
ones it must be said. And the old sense of a fullness
is here, though only lightly sketched in.

AUTUMN ON THE THRUWAY

Say that my arm is hurting.
Say that there are too many buts in the sky today.
Say that we need each other off and on to see how it feels.

After which we'll promise to see to it, see that it
Doesn't happen this way again so that we may
Do something about it when it does happen.

Or that sincerity cover us with a cloak of shame
While our clothes are drying by the campfire this night
Of nights that means to go on and prepackage some of the original flame

In order to sell it so as to recoup some of the losses that
Started us on this path, repay the original investors.
How sweet then the bargain, the transaction. And you fear nothing

Notable, the skylight has been activated already.
Best to stay around admiring the new look on things.
Invent a new hat. Put on a growing season, staple the others

To the door hidden in the wilderness. And the losses be ours,
Not someone's in the sun, slut of some, weeping pointedly.
And the blinders—I have signed for them too.

Studies show it hanging in frost, in pajamas, up in the air
And a cerberus basks underneath, its own snowhole round
As an apple in belief. Water the tree in this area and it

Never expedites how much we were hoping to receive out of
What was promised originally, yes, traced on the tracing paper
Of some mood one day. We can never actually account for it

Or how lush its primitivism, in the beginning,
How steep the wall of its veil over face, or how
Far you had come, little

Spinner that that's all right now. How we come to be seen.
Yet we know we must pay

Not use up any money in between, for it

To become us, and then all lost, a second time
But in a time the merry neutral wisdom is gathered, to be sewed

Into the lining and you must cherish it there.
Never believe a false passport to the land of chocolate and bees'
Reasons and be forelost, freedom from a refuge
That took over once you began to get used to it. No, this other

Hand is the wish I bury and keep for you, really the only one
Beside me long, into a tense's dense conditions
And then you tear, tearing: O how long was it going to be for us

Until the scenery lay quiet like a beloved dog's head under the hand,

For what was moving to be moving, for it to have courted an aspirin
And lost face at the quarry edge. Hand me that theogony
And then get lost, don't read me my rights, please get out of here

Until I can think and then two more of us, for a day, come to where we two
Parted and it is on a day. I can't think
How it completes my thought but I never knew how that was going to begin.

Nor did it mean anything for anyone growing up then.
We were merely—"sentimental" about describes it, yet that can too be loving
In one's breath, provided other people also move around in it,

Disturbing it. It's no Volga but it's vast and dreary and it moves,
Keeps on moving. And so it is a show window at Christmas,
Brimming with lights, with more suggested memories than it could deal with, and we,

Well we help it along for our sakes, which is to say not very much.
We thought about it so often. How many figures I had rehearsed
In the garret where you could see your breath, whomping

My sides from the cold. Now, to have written it, merely,
Seems tepid, a kind of clashing conundrums thing, and
People walk out in the middle of it, rustling programs, tears spatter

The hateful embroidered lace, O why not tear off that Juliet cap and throw it
With the papers of dubious cleanliness, anything so
As to avoid the recrimination of a look that says you did just what you did,

No other, and how is it now for you. Stupid spruces tremble at
Stucco corners and why is this not to be attributed to the hand
Of some vengeful but well-meaning deity too? Why are we alone

Held responsible for the way everything gets to look, why are we admonished
Every time we walk out and see things starting to be the way again
They probably were in the near past, just yesterdays ago, when we haven't changed,

Only coarsened, merely from staying around a few too many seconds, an expression
That hardens while the photographer tries to focus on it, that's enough
For today, this day at least. And how much farther he tries to follow when you

Have passed under the willows' swinging garlands, past the sweep
Of the stream where you sink in up to the ankles, on to the drought and out,
And he says, what a fine time, why how much to be here,

Only you don't come round. Please send somebody to finish
Or our nails may be chipped, our locusts blighted, our hoarfrost dispelled by a breath
That who wants to enjoy the risk of? Not him. Not me, certainly,

Though what you ask for is not infrequently what you get.
Under an upturned cartwheel hat she looked up, so solemnly silly
That for a moment you had to forget to outtake her. And her drink needed replenishing.

So in the long run all of it takes us far from the sea of what we were as individuals
And more from the time when all that mattered, mattered as to a single
Individual too old for the part, though a pair. Now it's possible to see

How far apart we were on most issues, and the European cooks it differently,
Besides, and set against the plainness of American lives it melts like a wall and
Rivulets, runnels drain off it as though from a roof, rushing to join you

In the gutter, and where the growing begins askance
This time. No more frankness, it is apt to cloud, to
Give off steam in the time it takes to distinguish one accent from the truth.

So the lovely second theme is somewhat marred
By buried memories of revenge, and when the time comes to
Reinvent the initial phase, why, all but grinning stupidly, it hands

Its cards to another player and takes off in the direction of the pond.
Wait! But another's daring solution will never rescue twice the omen
That hankered for more polity, and beside us though we were of no mind

To reckon it into what we were being elaborated by. Myrtles fall,
Crape drapes. The spear
Is slowly lowered as for the last curtain.

You've got to decide what your name is going to be,
What to do about it. By what ring we are decoded. Tangles
Of snake-grass and more, though it wouldn't

Do to talk about it, would it? Why, since I have come home from school,
Why must I intend it? Who is the person who wants this? How many
Guests has he invited, where do they come from? Who isn't

In on the trail? Now his men have departed. They have been sent away. Does that
Mean they won't be back? Do we ever avoid our own reckoning, even
When the moist, mild sky smiles and the portcullis is up,

The drawbridge lowered, the road delighted to wind
Into a newly dapper landscape, pointedly new, and it runs away
With us, sweeps us up into something, some way to be

With pleasure and not be too long about it so the mood stays
But isn't fixed? If only I'd known what I was getting into
That day in Arizona, I'd have taken another detour, but you see

When you see gravel, you think roadbed, automatically, forgetting how little
It takes to set anybody off, buzzing into dreams. Old papers and
Memoirs. Feet under the desk. A tiny girl who smiles and is prepared.

What year was that? Who was in power then? By what
Sin have we been burned? And did the president point
His pointer at the blackboard to the word "articulate," and did

Those feet reiterate the premise, damp down through the ages, fresh, yes,
But so ancient, like an ague. Teeth chattering, all proceeded to the dump.
After all, it would be time soon.

After all, nobody knows how to make this any more. You can't
Find us in their lounges. Soon, soon, however, the overpass takes us home.
The leaves are spent, lying in a ditch. Girls gone. The music, the horses took off.

THE LITTLE BLACK DRESS

All that we are trying most defiantly to unravel
is waiting, close to the path. Yes,
but the pace is both relaxed and insistent,
a swimming up from under. Your plan sounds fine.

I knew a brunette once in Omaha,
he said, and that struck us as news. He hadn't
been out of the truck long. On the dank ground the new
willow leaves lay, a reproof to him and us.
Why can't the clay bind us more firmly still,
until he can read,
get something out of these notations that arrive
every day, like letters, O not in the empty house.

PART OF THE SUPERSTITION

Help, when it came, came from an unexpected place.
It was so nice he couldn't sleep. Our rooms darken
with every new place of experience. All roses
admit this, and life stays on, fidgeting, their dream
disappointed, on the run, and it's your fault,
who never had the courage to know nothing and simultaneously
be attentive. That's where the secret comes in,
and, as you might expect, it's quite unhandy,
especially if you're in a coma. Now I don't want
to have to speak to you again; we're on the way down,
that much is assured, and leggy growth has to stop somewhere,
at least it did in my day. About what colors to buy:
this is something each dean and priest decides
for himself, and then they melt and turn into the jackpot,
which is a little disturbing. Don't squirm,
however, there are other houses on this road to peace
we can actually live in, as a snail its shell,
or bird pants. Then a calend grabs your hand
and tugs you into the future, and that's about all the space
there is left. Wipe your nose. Don't fudge
the horizon or it will come clattering down
on us like the earthquake at Lisbon, but always,
be brave. Yet these are old wives' tales,
in truth; nothing insists you believe in them
except as dreams, which permeate the background
of our day like colored raindrops, and so go away
before too long. Many have turned back
at this point; the trials, the trails, are thistles,
inherently unrewarding. Yet those who wish to play
say many are pleased to be in that day:
pleased, and not a little scared, but from where
will peace come if not from those beetling crags?

So many varied stimuli, and I
was nigh to frantic, as it may believe you,
and has for other hosts. Yet these passions, arrayed
like infantry, continue to absorb and confuse
by turns. No use shouting about waste, it was
a necessary corner in your apartment that couldn't be filled
by anything but its own besottedness. And we think, when we
do play, that a special aggravation
has sunk its beak in us like Prometheus' eagle,
yet all proceeds from an inability and desire to win
leading to narrow channels and bogus expectations.
Cut short the customary peroration:
its wings soar o'er us still, or will be, and we, we'll
have a hand in sorting them out, strand
by tinted strand, and be sure a life will arise swollen from this:
a vacant place in the story. My glory
when it comes will resemble yours in its feinting
and the way it orders waiters with soiled aprons around.
We can be back for much of it. Haste, arise;
a big thing is happening to everyone. We were so prudent
in our clothes back there it got forgotten, blurred
with the wet lawn. And when the president
looked out his window he saw it, and ran to tell the vice-president,
and so a compact was kept. I sure wish
it were possible to pole oneself more than a few feet off this shore,
but it seems to want us. And I can't explain how a muskrat
would ever know about such a thing, yet it did.

So there were times in between like the seasons
and the times between them when peaches fall,
and dancers sift across the stage like leaves,
and these are dark times. Only remember that the figure
worked deep into the fabric implodes there;
has a next, a resting place. It is from the multiplication
of similar wacko configurations that theses do arise
to attest the efficacy of this castor oil,

this medicine. And if why we want to go away
is as plain as the nose on your face, the buried village,
cut out of rose-petal limestone, is still standing. Haply
some faith trickles out of it, and is not lost
in the glittering grass, but persists to become a torrent,
then a turret, somewhere else. For there is a key,
and it leads to your door. Yet it is only repetition, something
the seasons like a lot. And as you get up to go you mutter,
and that's it!—the fortunate crisis that was always
going to stave us off, and explain so much
about car wrecks, and postage stamps and the like.
Farewell in the rain; it is surely lucky to know
as much as we do, and not to know as much
as we do. Or were taught was proper. Papers
will explain it, music it. That's a promise.

THE ART OF SPEEDING

And when some sidle awkwardly,
why, the grove is green again. There is more than enough catfood
for two, she said. And I think I belong in this prism.
Day means more than luck itself to me,
but I shall be forgotten
on a shore made monotonous by the inverted hulls of rowboats.
There is more than enough time for me,
sympathy too. I'm the cap and bells that don't belong.
A free-lance artist. The last and first of the romantics.

Sometimes a suppler season weaves pliant straws
into a crown for no one in particular.
This hiatus is my legacy:
a patterned map whose symmetries invite exploration
yet in the end repel the cold traveler, wrapped
in gray at the end of the mole.
He sees farther into the rising banister of the city's rage
and shuts out all ivory memories like pestilence.
Indeed he is the naked forager.

But when tomatoes are ripe and girls
don't mind, and the sun is civil again, then
look in your shoeboxes for sheaves of snapshots
that came over us and were here, wild as the wilderness.
We forgot who was talking to us on the quay.
It just might have been a distinguished stranger.
Now his visor keeps us from noticing
his general appearance, but genially we all say
how much we have loved this place, how gay
are the receipts. All we have to do is stay.

Yet more pictures are involved than the accountant
realizes, moaning over his headache: sometimes it agrees
with us to say we do. And then the game is darker;
no one pauses in the rain.

AMERICAN BAR

We bake a dozen kinds of muffins every day
yet we are cold and disquieting at heart.
I fear for his sciatica, though
we were never lovers.
Let me memorialize this mattress, M.
le Comte, he will be decent
in this fog that emanates from everything
though the air is fresh and sunny. Thought
about wandering down to the river to have a
look at the water. It always has so much to say,
more than the upended rain barrel in its day
had. See the monkey in its cage.
Bright eyes are feasting again and again.

In the casual track of a zipper my penis
once got stuck, and it's been like that ever since:
feet stop where no snare lives, the best
is to die down and desist. Perhaps life is better
near the Arctic Circle, where the buildings are plain
and no trees sing. One can feel totally indoors.
The wireless plays a lanky tune;
there are spots on the wall from the moisture
you either keep out or keep in. I forget which,
and what a bird looks like. The winter night drones on
for centuries, and what keeps us at peace is actually
the sight of an empty cage
and a few children's drawings of it.

My, we have raced to be equivocally here
and have invented what sign? Off of what do we climb

to the lower level, what compact fleet of stairs
is nestled here? Or did we bowdlerize each other's delirium
in fear of having the last word, and it frightened *us* off the page?
In any case have a ripping good time. The boars
will be here around then, as you know.

FROM PALOOKAVILLE

"Death cancels all engagements."
—Clifton Webb, in the movie *Laura*

The midgets stand on giants who stand on midgets
in Palookaville
that day of storm notwithstanding and it still takes one
on out to the "farther reaches" where boys play and maids bay
at the moon
in my Palookaville
where the stench of farts drenches outside irony with the dust of snow
where all is served up right
to blond kids in history books on the gothic outskirts
where everything gets unravelled just right
where you can see a coincidence coming for miles down the valley
along the trestle when the snow the femurs the cries
demur and act unwise
at a time when centers shatter in strict unison
when doubt is in the call of the fox
and the sunsets are like weddings

I came here of my own accord
from Djakarta
I'm as old as you are and dare to say so
but the falling liaisons spat out like miles of thread
are the lining of time's one easy lesson
the shocks deep and narrow like crevasses dog teams fly over
over and around
aiming no way to please
and it does in the arrested quickness of the visit, task—
even life is the least bit pejorative
but not the costumes the calendar
the trivia the painted trappings

to come undone
in your embrace and that's the word

You were sent for and that is all
no word on why some became
the anvil
and from here all that runs is dust
or consommé there was fear smeared again on the walk
and for two consecutive days
we go out on it it's pretty safe
so far
on the fifth day a bank fails there are great falls
and iodine in the little house
it smells more like an accord this time
and then there were birds you know too soft
this time for much
of an answer
and they came were there under steel arcades
the night brings its business along
stalls as though a feint saved the day one
other time and now it's horses all around for anybody that thinks
they've got a contusion or a monopoly
surely it was warm faces all round

The accents are distant as bells in that other hometown
the stories often gory
tell why please the accents and your own personal vignette came up
without a number and no one explained the cause
a dim musicale in some small room
folded under netting as though the crows stood by
to watch
under the felt cushion something impolite zoomed
it was suggested that we all carry away
our traces that we dispose of them "thoughtfully"
so as not to leave any bones of an argument around
for others mauling traces

in bushes
black ones riding with white snow a pure, defined drop
of atheism and it arches out too wide, too near the circumference
of the pier too much to say for what an old man did
on a recent day and what if it comes round
on a recent day and what if we all did
and who shoved the pace of the thermometer
on an outing who shamed the toaster
who is to say

ANOTHER EXAMPLE

Of our example, earth,
we know the star-shaped universe:
divisions,
         somewhere,
                of July streets.
Is it a bucket you sit in
             or on?
How they led us past the fence.
The one horse was mortified.

But it's unhealthy, you say
we must have another example,
just one.

What's wanted is faces in windows
screams that went away a long time ago.
What says to recall them?

To be revived like paper ants
and then endure the long vacuum of pre-eternity
and still be allowed to buy something
on the station platform?

The train is turning away—
There are no familiar quotations.

Here, put some on a plate, he said. That's the way.

AVANT DE QUITTER CES LIEUX

They watch the blue snow.
It is the fifth act in someone else's life,
but here, on Midway Island, reefs and shoals interfere
with that notion. That nothing so compact
as the idea of a season is to be allowed
is the note, for today at least. It is Tuesday morning.
They sing a duet of farewell
to their little table, and to themselves as they were
when they sat at it. Noon intersects with fat birds
the rhythm of dishes in the cupboard. My love,
he seems to say, is this the way it is for you? Then we shall have to leave
these shabby surroundings for others, but first
I want to plant a kiss like a star
on your forehead. The ships are knocking together at the quayside,
the lanyards struck, there is more moving
than we were intended for, as we clear out
nodding to the caryatids we pass. Perhaps they will sing to us.

And in a summer house somewhere in Russia
a clematis soaks up the heat. One can think without breathing
of the blue snow that invades the fields, a curse some obscure ancestor
once let fall and now it's the custom, duly serenaded each season
before the apples rust
and the idea of winter takes over, to be followed in short order
by the real thing.
If all of us could lead lives of razoring things out of the newspaper,
filing them on pincushions . . . but no. There is the father
and morning to be dealt with, and after that the students arrive.
The rhythm is broken up among them.
That was a cold year, but not
the last. It will be remembered.

Why is it you always ask me this, and this:
is there no question behind the arras of how we now meet
seconding each other's projects, our emotions? Or is that too weak
as a question, though strong enough as an affirmation, so that we again go out
from each other. One shades one's eyes automatically, though the sky
is dark. "We have no place to go" (the fifteenth
major situation), and if God decrees we like each other, someday
we will meet on a stone up there, and all will not be well,
but that is useful. Great rivers run into each other and graves
have split open, the tyranny of dust plays well, there is
so little to notice. Besides we have always known each other.

Except for that it was automatically the century
before this one. Thus we are made aware of the continuity
of times that were, and time itself is revealed
not as a series of rooms but a single corridor
stretching into the truth: an alpine pasture, with a few goats
and, in the distance, a hovel. It is high noon. Dinorah,
who has lost her goat, sings the mad scene for which her life
has been a preparation, sings it out of daylight, out of the outcropping
of rock overhead, out of the edelweiss and cowslips.
Now it is the turn of the mountain god
but he refuses to play. The blue snow returns. Shopfronts are boarded up.

Still one should never be in a hurry to end, to contrast the ending
with the articulations that have gone before. True, these are merely space,
but one in which lives can take on a single and sparing sharpness
that is an education in itself. This is one life
as we thought it over, and there are other songs, some too true to mention,
others of little weight, optional, cut from most editions
but waiting silently in place where they are expected.
The story falls, mountains conspire, brooks hesitate,
the storm endures.

THE WHITE SHIRT

Suddenly all is quiet again.
I want to talk about something.
It's not that easy. Pay no attention.

No amount of conservation affects
the wrinkled gourd. The dry shore.
A combustion engine
means it's not working.

Thing of the past,
you in your limits,
growing,
my working place.
The band is up.

But if it wasn't for changes,
where would we go? Just
having the illusion is enough.
But charge them for it;
serve immediately.

BAKED ALASKA

I /
It will do. It's not
perfect, but it will do
until something better comes along.

It's not perfect.
It stinks. How are we
going to get out of having it
until something comes along, some ride
or other? That will return us
to the nominative case, shipshape and easy.

O but how long are you going to wait
for what you are waiting for, for
whatever is to come? Not
for long, you may be sure.
It may be here already.
Have you checked the mailbox today?

Sure I have, but listen.
I know what comes, comes.
I am prepared
to occupy my share of days,
knowing I can't have all of them. What is, is
coming over here to find you
missing, all or in part. Or you read me
one small item out of the newspaper
as though it would stand for today.
I refuse to open your box of crayons. Oh yes, I know
there may be something new in some combination
of styles, some gift in adding the addled
colors to our pate. But it's just too mush
for me. It isn't that I necessarily

set out on the trail of a new theory
that could liberate us from our shoes as we walked.
It's rather that the apartment comes to an end
in a small, pinched frown of shadow. He walked
through the wood, as a child. He will walk
on somebody's street in the days that come after.
He's noted as a problem child, an ignoramus;
therefore why can you not accept him in
your arms, girdled with silver and black
orchids, feed him everyday food?

Who says he likes cuttlebone?
But you get the idea, the idea
is to humor him for what vexations
may hatch from the stone attitude
that follows and clears the head, like a sneeze.
It's cozy to cuddle up to him,
not so much for warmth as that brains
are scarce, and two will have to do.
It takes two to tango,
it is written, and much
in the way of dragons' teeth after that,
and then the ad hoc population that arises
on stilts, ready to greet or destroy us, it
doesn't matter which, not quite yet, at least.

Then when the spent avenger
turns tail you know it had all to do with
you, that discharge of fortunes
out of firecrackers, like farts. And who's to say
you don't get the one that belongs to you?

But he speaks, always, in terms of perfection,
of what we were going to have
if only he hadn't gotten busy and done something about it, yea,
and turned us back into ourselves

with something missing. And as oarsmen
paddle a scull downstream with phenomenal speed,
so he, in his cape, queries:
Is the last one all right? I know
I keep speaking of the last one, but is it all right?
For only after an infinite series
has eluded us, does the portrait
of the boy make sense, and then such a triangular one:
he might have been a minaret, or a seagull.
He laid that on the car's radiator
and when you turned around it is gone.

II /

Some time later, in Provence,
you waxed enthusiastic about the tail
piece in a book, gosh how they
don't make them like that in this century, any more.
They had a fiber then that doesn't exist now.
That's all you can do about it.
Sensing this, in the sopping diaspora, many a tanglefoot
waits, stars bloom at scalloped edges
of no thing, and it begins to
bleed, like a bomb or bordello.
The theme, unscathed,
with nothing to attach it to.

But like I was saying, probably some of us were encouraged
by a momentary freshness in the air
that proved attractive, once we had dwelt in
it, and bathed for many years
our temples in its essence. Listen, memory:
do this one thing for me
and I'll never ask you again for anything else:
just tell me how it began! What
were the weeds that got caught in the spokes
as it was starting up, the time the brakeshaft split

and about all the little monsters that were willing to sit
on the top of your tit, or index finger.
How in the end sunshine prevailed—
but what was that welling in between?
those bubbles
that proceeded from nowhere—surely there must be a source?
Because if there isn't it means that we haven't paid
for this ticket, and will be stopped at the exit-gate
and sent back on a return journey through ploughed fields
to not necessarily the starting place, that house
we can hardly remember, with the plangent
rose-patterned curtains.

And so in turn he who gets locked up is lost
too, and must watch a boat nudge the pier
outside his window, forever, and for aye,
and the nose, the throat will be stopped
by absolutely correct memories of what did
we think we were doing when it all began happening,
down the lanes, across vales, out into the open city street.

And those it chooses can always say
it's easy, once you learn it, like a language,
and can't be dislodged thereafter.
In all your attractive worldliness, do you consider
the items crossed off the shopping list,
never to breathe again until the day
of bereavement stands open and naked like a woman
on a front porch, and do those you hobnob
with have any say or leverage in the matter?
Surely it feels like a child's feet propel us along

until everyone can explain.
Hell, it's only a ladder: structure
brought us here, and will be here when we're

honeycombs emptied of bees, and can say
that's all there is to say, babe; make it a good one
for me.

III /
And when the hectic
light leaches upward into rolls of dark cloud,
there will no longer be a contrast between thinking
and daily living. Light will be something even,
if remorseful, then. I say, swivel
your chair around, something cares, not the lamps purling
in the dark river, not the hot feet on the grass,
nor the cake emerging from the oven, nor the silver
trumpets on the sand: only a lining
that dictates the separation of this you from this some other,
and, in memorializing, drools. And if the hospice
gets over you this will be your magpie, this old hat,
when all is said, and done. No coffee, no rolls—
only a system of values, like the one printed
beside your height as it was measured as you grew
from child to urchin to young adult
and so on, back into the stitched wilderness
of sobs, sighs, songs, bells ringing, athirst
for whatever could be discerned in the glacier:
tale, or tragedy, or talc, that backlit
these choices before we learned to talk,
and so is a presence now, a posture like a chimney
that all men take to work with them
and that all see with our own eyes just
as the door is shutting, O shaft of light, O excellent, O irascible.

PRIVATE SYNTAX

The obligation I have assumed is an unprepossessing one.
I'll be glad to get back to the city of painted scenery

and horse-drawn carts, before resuming the march toward
new standards of equality. Rain washes in the chimney;

the immense task-force that drew us out into unwise confidences
repeats the crescendo in neon: this is about as sanguinary

as it gets, so why tremble on the edge? Leap, if you must,
only don't blame the processus for what you brought on yourself,

tarring others too with the brush of a rabid potential music
that cares for itself and dislikes oil-aureoled puddles

as much as it does human experimentation. Whose style degrades your
ruminating on it all until you think you've come up with something:

anything, don't share it. Don't be special, silly or civil.
In time grapes fatten. Waves accept one more chore, or shore,

and everything gets done, is distributed equally into your plan
of reducing the workload and actually making some money, for a change.

NOT NOW BUT IN FORTY-FIVE MINUTES

Anyway, sleep came that day
not so that you'd notice
what was silhouetted against what—was it the pillow or the bags
over by that glass of water?
I mean we're not getting into androgyny?
You better believe it. Those towers say
the gift of day is wholesale
to men
under the awning, the annoyed shopkeeper's
gesture of putting something right
after you've touched it can be
believed

No it was an altogether more interesting case.
We often said throw out the baby with the bathwater
eavesdroppers seldom hear good of themselves
the plant stinks
lick honey through a cleft stick.
Other than that it is no premise to you
in time it will be calm be gay
stay away from others' questions
they will have you before time too
with the pilgrim's classic good taste
I'm spattered I am brunch

I know how to solve
you I love you
with that the cat
walked last into an open barrier
neither time nor spires were demeaning

I know I planned
it me to be

all over you
I thank a thousand dunces for this webbed, precious
gift of knowledge
to no man's height I am authorized
to stay here after the handcuffs
and the lard I am chilled
by the reflection
of you

and the stain stays
It was on the beautiful part
must now be read with it
I am all apple
to thank
you

No one knows what we do when we're apart
A veil veins the days of our separate living
when we're in trouble we're back in class
but now to do those tedious sums
requires having loved and in the course of it
shrugged
and if they came by that schoolhouse on such-and-such a day
everything would be normal from the dozing stove
to the pillar of milk on the door

and we should all get together afterward
put our other concerns
on the table
and we should all french kiss get elected
not to be trouble
to stand up in reason's roar

IN ANOTHER TIME

Actually it was because you stopped,
but there was no need to,
the forest wasn't too dark, and yet,
you stopped and then went on a little way
as though to embarrass the idea of stopping.
By then the everything
was involved in night:
cars were discharging patrons in front of theaters
where light swelled, then contracted
into tiny slivers. Then listened.

A kind of powdered suburban poetry fits
the description, and isn't
precisely it. There was no briskness,
yet things got quickly done.
The cartoon era of my early life
became the printed sheaves and look:
what's printed on this thing?
Who knows what it's going to be?
Meanwhile it gasps like a fish on a line.

It is no doubt a slicker portrait
than you could have wished, yet all
the major aspects are present:
there you bent down under the waterfall
as though to read little signs
in the moss and it all came to life
but quietly. There is no way to transcribe it.

WITHERED COMPLIMENTS

Have a care lest
the jewelled words of others
force you to act, you too: "Delicious.
I love you. Goodbye." For in that autumn
after speech strange desires stir.
It is not enough
to have kept one's hands to oneself,

not enough to see them cheating
and take no action. It is not enough,
finally, to turn
and walk back to the house
where disappointed parents wait, not
enough to smile through abuse and gather them
into the big, hectic embrace.

These days there are other worries to assess.
How did that band of shrubbery grow so sharp
that the rest of the landscape is dim,
pleading ignorance? And the arborist has other
things on his mind, as does the land-surveyor.
If you too could see that far out to sea
your forces might crumble. They, though,
take it in stride, but that too might be a warning:
earth, air, tire, water,

let all stand, be around
as much as we wrap around them
at day's outer limits.
A kind of slow afternoon here, too.
The aftershock holds no surprises.

THE WIND TALKING

Faithful I keep coming over to address the issues,
the ills no man can stomach, or anything that *feels* warm,
less bumptious and froward perhaps, speeding,
on wounded calendar, and faithful you coming to me ouch
plans pleasure no person can resist, the time
to roll out of bed, run out the white door, into the sickness
of the apt. Approach. Wait—
too many trees are tied to this, for desire's
ambitions to become known. I'll say to you
how usually around you are and my coming frequently
fits. Young warriors are aghast—no one
had foreseen it. That just keeps making book, into play,
the play of the weather, where snowballs flew across the stage.
The cast was furious. Don't explain, there's nothing you can do
except stay out of harm's way, waiting, in a doorway—
I like you here, and by the woodpile, and think
it's after something, but no one came. And the door was slightly ajar,
too, it could be considered closed. Some welcome! Maybe
you are older and more spirited than I think, let's
have a try, go on, the crab missile told
how it was all just plain dust and guts. Any can hold him,
I've tried, and now you are back. The volume
of his chant extended me, to be with you, falling off, in the life.

Night promontories can be sticky there is a whole other suite of
glabrous thingamabobs adhering to the minutes of my vacuum.
Then to get down and crawl it, into the unimagined spaces that
were, it's true, there. I still address it. Like a lost man.
The oldest sewer in captivity. I can shrink it too,
and desperately bawling you knows no man's coming to lick it,
be beside it, extrapolate us on the ledge. We're caring.
Shoo, that's all-important now. Under the legs
of this chair I can see into the runnels. Midnight's near.

Let's doff with the clothes, lay on burlap
over granite. Ssh. He hears. The mouse's wits list
all somebody isn't going to tell us about the improbable
financial backing of the adventure just as it sinks. The lights
go out at sea. Try a waltz then.
The disease of timing's etched itself into the very skull
of the churl as plodding she shifts from Yule berries
to centerpiece, nothing more's in my craw.
How did I come over the last time? I'm all confused.
Besides, you got me when I was just out, and you were all going to say
I waited, plaited at the formal garage, all despair
and too tidy to come out. But I do. I'm like the
bashful bull, my bicycle has hindsight, my ass is clean,
I'm being raked over the coals by an uncertain
hand ceremoniously, the curtain's a riot, it could all

be badly blistered. Look, I have a vacuum cleaner.
In the janitor's hand some prurient
fun must be planned and I'll go where the washer decides me
into small dovecot openings that are for the birds. Please,
accept kindly the running board of my road
to you, the lucky dusk that was over Fifth Avenue. They chanted
variously, the lights separated into grave reminders.
Well I am coming up too and don't much like
your progress with the waves. Seems they are dividers,
or something, something that was cherished long before
you and the odious others came to think about it.
Come to think of it I know that man's name, but not his station, but I am
working on all those orders. If we have to come, he can come.

Meanwhile before the fire one putters and absorbs so much
of the floor it's like returning to a natural Elysium
one was meant never to have left. So long, it's so dry
in the dells that dust can't get accepted and we three
under the umbrella of stars shout down the well into the next
performance, which will be more varied.

I'm so glad the tocsin assimilated all the calls to order that must have
been found wanting under one odoriferous tree or another, it's all
the same, sample. My britches are wanting suspenders
and I too want, where it wanders, under regular
bridges and pavements. We seem to buy flowers
but are erased from death, it passes over
into the lovely material of the sky I get used to wearing.
The man I love is ready here in the faceless backrooms
under ground and by his shining, in the trees of heaven too,
a final note. Gorged and empty. Dissatisfied,
yet rolling in sleep's tresses as never, and in front of a junction
of light to lunar light, to folds of earth's sleep.
He's one to know. You'll all wear me out. I'm green and gray;
the current is voiceless and occasionally.

JOY

Think of it as some god-liberating whimsy
that heaven and the emperor's mice detain
in the province of boredom. The signor's wrath
is cold at these times, to nail the fizzle, explain
exactly what went wrong in clear, easy-to-understand
sentences. Besides, an imperfect embrace continues
from the past like an organ-point. So it was not you
in the original documents attributed to "I,"
and was no safer to pursue our advantage albeit
a mild one. The scene is classical;
the last twister corrodes into terror.

To be living on this scale. An old drum
collapses like ash. Seek it tomorrow
in the diversity of sleep,
the promised landscape.

IRRESOLUTIONS ON A THEME OF LA ROCHEFOUCAULD

"We are all strong enough to bear the misfortunes of others."

We leave out old regrets
that when they be found are almost blended
in the grass, shadows of apple stems
they might be or collages from another country.
We shall, at the steeps, commandeer all
that bed is good for, then sink into a platter of sleep.

Bringing water to the fountain, a hot day's
rest, and too soon is it excluded
to the delight of those sitting near us, who,
on the verge of bailing out, decided to approach
the argument again in a spirit of fairness this time
since we all have to cooperate, or else the earth
will get slightly out of kilter, its revolutions
a few seconds off, enough to produce climatic changes
in places you least think of—

One day the mice became suspicious. That was all
we needed to get going again, in plans
of luxurious travel this time—on foot, by plane
aching through the deserted night for its
imagined double, shot against the sunrise
with blips to read by, a miracle—

One should be filling out
the forms, but tension has lessened, though
we need to know we live in explosive times;
we can see our way around corners to where
we dressed the birds. They liked the clothes
we gave them, liked us, but still they
wanted to go home, not to a forest

or savannah, but to the place of captivity
they had always known, a cage somewhere inside a school.
So each day the predicament
emerges different, yet the same—you want
to have birds at your shoulders and wrists, to connive
with nature in her song, but something always
leaves you. Suddenly there are no more disappointments to be had
and the laziest are crowned and anointed for their efforts:
somewhere we see in this something which is shyly wrong,
some corner of the heart, bird-
haunted, by birdsong haunted, as though we two
were far away, and these others strangely near—
a paradise, if we had the facts to open it.

And when an elf
sits on a golf tee before you, and someone
behind you asks to play through: then, then
it doesn't matter much which of the old gypsy crones is
really a princess in disguise, with flowing
chocolate braids, and olive-dusted complexion! O may she
redress our wounds, and leave
connivance to us, where we shall find
it a suitable burial ground and all
will be as if we never had lied,
never hounded our mortal parents with persistent questions
and all shall be as though dawn came easily
any time. The mountains fall apart
in my hand as I hold you: there, three
are smoothed over already with
five more to come before a delicious breakfast,
and I try to cherish you.

A CALL FOR PAPERS

It buttered no parsnips that it was raining
on some statues of older men. The call had gone out
and from all across the country, papers
kept blowing in. The little crazy guy converged
with a very interesting man who was right here
in an antique perspective:
The appetites were enormous, the provisions limitless.
Fifteen read their papers
last year at this time, the group said.
In the case of Boston-Cleveland or Hartford-Philadelphia
you don't get arrested for heavily kicking a sign.
But as daffodils and raindrop-preludes fall
from the symbol-laden heavens, you can be charged
for forgetting,
for ignoring the very basement of your and others'
ideas until they come at you like stray cats
and it isn't *their* fault. Remember that.

The scale descends
to a kind of landing, then descends some more.
Cooler heads prevailed
and something that the work was not resembling
gave you a distaste for discovery.
Whether I'm fooling around or not it is incumbent
on the brothels of history to raise up their sheets
and vote with a bean for or against capital punishment.
Don't you see
it's the only way to measure
the zebras moving to warn us,
reptiles in rep ties at the pass?
Carry on, crow.
Meanwhile sleep binds us lightly
so that we can easily slip away as the season

approaches on tortoise feet. Around the corner
of midnight, and a thousand miles away this morning?
What good are hygrometers, and what men need us
more than they need air or defense?

We'll see you at the end of the month! they cried.
Small waves broke as they re-formed
across the bay's lumpy waters
in time for this session and for the next
one and for the one after that.

LOVE'S OLD SWEET SONG

Because if all of life is just a blip or some kind of exclamation
mark at the bottom of last week's weather (an almost snow-filled
field from which some weeds extrude; should we persist in
trying to find a home for these?), it means, doesn't it, that we're
allowed to backtrack to the slough we were backsliding into
anyway, and really learn about ourselves from it this time? I mean a
quagmire's a tidy place for pausing between highballs; there is
so much more to everything but this is a not inconsiderable prison
yard for getting that all-important exercise.
                                    Meantime, one comes
bearing an envelope that is fresh and blue; one salivates; even
if it's not a stay of execution but an order for the immediate putting-into-
effect of same, there's something to learn. It's not like two cats
ignoring each other in a basement areaway. By that I mean it was
going to lead up to something and then did, quite quickly. Better
than scanning hirsute sands for plumes announcing the arrival
of reinforcements; in those cases one invariably skips forward to a
time in the near future when everybody is happy again and an engagement
ring slips onto a ring finger of its own accord. But back,

I say, the heck with endings. I don't think I want to wear those socks.
On any other day of the week my attitude would elicit a few stares;
my value-judgments are like what they used to call an "overdressed"
woman, and it has come about that my shadow is invisible to me, but
I don't know this yet. The conventional wisdom is that we
desire what's unattainable (reclining clouds, distant factory chimneys)
for precisely that reason. No allowance is made for the goodness
that might be lurking therein, like love in a tongue-tied child
whose cheek one pinches as one passes along to bigger and better
disappointments. We never know what we could walk back to except
when we do go back, and then it's as if not knowing and knowing
were the same thing.
                  I long for more weather around us,

but it's just not going to happen till we're in the middle
of its happening and know the results without being able to see them.
The time for passing is past and none but an idiot would think otherwise.
Yet I see I shall be needing some appraisals, tall and lucky
totems foundered in taller grass.

WILD BOYS OF THE ROAD

"Why, there's the well where the message fell apart:
its rusted chain gleams still. And there's the happy one,
so little she was excused from most occasions.
The blinkered sun circles it now, the last act,
noting how little its motions will be called on the carpet
(or it will fade the carpet), with the resulting freedom to act
like a knife, or a snake in the night. When it's all over
we say I could drink it now and then,
about three times a week. But the heavenly uproar
is heavier; storms mean business
in this day and age. The only viable
mode is to walk out; you'll find the slick streets keep time
with your advancing to what is really seen when it is sold.

"Fresh air will have noticed the pond waterfall, how
the trillium darted out from underneath but
had nothing to say, no excuse for being there,
though perhaps one for what was there before, as a henchman's
eyelids close just before the deep fact of one
sitter's enduring, to pass the test, and then
everything is all right; the sun seems to have shifted
its position, allowing gray skies, crazy boys to bloom
all over the place, and yet we are here, safe, unsleeping,
perjured to a man but that's
what gets removed I guess. You have to
return to the old. And age builds it shining new for you.
We have too many things to think about
not to notice the dull horseman's color of coming
back to check once again. Besides, the lilac
flavor of after-shave stood up, grew him a new one,
and all cattle, all sentries were dispersed from the yard.
It's hard being in an epic but harder still
to hold on to the thread as it whips like a kite-string,

and some of us do get our deposit back. But for the most part
there is only land and that is obvious,
too near the lunar chasm to be depended on
and too smart not to give us the slip
as the occasion warrants."

When all is said and done we avoid our friends
not from fear of us but from a holy desire
not to cause a commotion. Poor boy, you thought
to have sipped from the center would be such an easy, exact thing,
like kneeling in church. But you see now how the watchman
destroys whatever it is one happens to be made of, purloins
the bulging eyes of expectation, leaving
curious pebbles in their place, or better
yet, no things, nothing of which the touch
can be determined: strange, elliptical events
with no name for them in the glossary. How the vegetation
would take over now: we'd be stalled again, the bad
smell on the verge of happening once again, the tin
posy in the doorjamb as unconcerned as if this
were a hundred and fifty years ago. Something has got to stop,
yet I tell you the enemies are for us, shouting in our ears.
The leaves are too little at the top,
and the years, well they come to seem little too, little and nifty,
though I suppose not for long, and I seem to hear
something will wring us, wrench us from the extremes
of piety on the one hand and salacious diffidence on the other: just
enough for the sing-song to get along, as we were,
nice and easy for us, stone plinths with fringe of grass.

LE MENSONGE DE NINA PETROVNA

This slave brings me tea,
and happy, I sit for a moment, a spare
moment. Time under the tree passes,
and those things which I have left undone
find me out! O my spirit shall be
audited! and unknown readers
grasp the weight of my words
as their feathery hulls blow away
leaving the crabbed and sullen seed
behind. And how many of these shall grow?
Really I thought it was autonomous
as the birds' song, the vultures' sleep,
under crags to whom virtuous
dreams come and torture them awake:

all alone lest someone
approach too near, in a fever
that binds the edge of sleep
where it blurs to hysterical necessity,
in these hours I am someone.
A patch of damp cannot ever overcome
the hurricane that blows where it wishes,
and the Christmas tree ornaments may well be
dispersed, that look so perfect,
hanging together,
as must we all, to the distant cheering
of high-school students at a game
who mean no harm
but their kind words cannot save us

or quite leave us alone
as one hand of the clock homes
in on its chosen numeral.

Costumes and memorized poems are the order
of this night
as through an enormous pastry tube
clouds ooze around the stars, lest
(so brittle and unimportant are they)
the wherewithal be lacking
to bring earth into some semblance
of unity under the sky
that mocks us and will never
let us be entirely
all that we were someday to be.

OF LINNETS AND DULL TIME

You said you don't want to know any more
than you do now, of every thing that might be
a person. It would be cheating. That is urgent.
If we are going to mean in so many ways
let them all be lopped off.
That way we'll know you're getting older.

I feel sorry for anyone that has to die.
The lines of what's expected
fan out like beaters. That's all,
I think. But I lose things, now.
The beautiful shape of the toilet interposed
a viability as the air-raid drill ended.
We've got to do something.
He may be up there now, trying to find us.
If you let me, I'll drive you back to the fairgrounds.

KOREAN SOAP OPERA

My sister and I don't seem to get along too well anymore.
She always has to have everything new in her house. Cherished ideals
don't suit her teal, rust and eggshell color scheme.
Of course, I was a buyer when she was still on the street
peddling the Communist Youth weekly. I have a degree
in marketing. Her boyfriend thinks I'm old-fashioned.
Well, I guess I do have an old-fashioned mentality.

What kind of a mentality
causes men to commit suicide in their air-conditioned glass boxes?
It has been a life of adjustments. I adjusted to the postwar boom
though it broke up my family. Some took their honor to the mountains,
to live on wood and water. But the investment years
wrought havoc with the landscape. Everything is modular now, even the trees.

Under the dizzying parabolas of the railroad bridge, where the thud
of laundry mallets used to resound, the swiftly flowing
current is like green cream, like baize unfit for fulling.
So old are the ways,
for lunch one might select a large smelly radish.
In the streets, as always, there is a smell of frying fish
no one notices. The rain cannot make up its mind.
Other people like it other ways.

I need to interact with postal employees, civil servants, that sort of thing.
Just being asleep isn't enough.
I must cry out against injustice in whatever position
sleep overtakes me. Only then will I have understood what the world
and servants mean by self-abolishment, the key, it is said,
to success. To stand and contemplate the sea
is to comprehend part of the package. What we need, therefore,
is market gardens bringing a sense of time with them,

of this time, honed to razor-sharpness. Yet the whole
scheme is invisible to any shareholder, and so the feeling
lessens, the idea that a composite portrait
may not be so important after all takes over like the shoulder
of a mill-wheel, slogging patiently under water, then back
to the zenith, where the watchword presumably is.
In schools they teach things like plus and minus
but not in the gorge, not in boiling mud.
Area residents were jolted to find what in essence
was a large swamp, pythons and all, in their communal front yard.
To me, this is insensate. I cannot stand the wind at my back
making of me nothing, to be handed
over, in turn, to this
man, this man. For though he weathered patiently
the name, the one that occurs to all of us, he went out
and came in, not in the best interests of abundance;
not, it seems, being anything but about to fall.

Here's a paradox for you: if the men are segregated
then why are the women not?
If the rich can survive dust-storms thanks to their red-and-gold liveried
postilions, then you are playing with an alphabet here: nothing
you invent can be a plenipotentiary,
turn itself inside-out, radiate
iron spokes at the mini-landscape, and so side with a population
of bears, who knows? Who knows how much there can be
of any one thing if another one stops existing? And the word you give to this
man, this man, is cold,
fossil fuel.

One snorts in the laundry, another
is broken beside the bed. A third is suspended
in a baobab for all the sins
no one ever knew, for sins of omission are like pearls
next to the sin of not knowing, and being excused

for it. So it all comes round
to individual responsibility and awareness,
that circus of dusty dramas, denuded forests and car dealerships, a place
where anything can and does happen, and hours and hours go by.

A DRIFTWOOD ALTAR

I'll tell you what it was like:
If you could afford it, you could probably have had it,
no questions asked. If it ran well, hugged the road well,
cupped your body like a loose-fitting suit, there was only
the down payment; the rest is future memories.
Of all those who came near him at this stage, only
a few can describe him with any certainty: a drifter
was the consensus, polite with old people,
indifferent to children, extremely interested in young adults,
but so far, why remember him? And few did,
that much is certain. I caught up with him
on a back porch in Culver City, exchanged the requisite
nod, shirt biting into the neck. How is it with you and some
who have no meaning, to whom nothing pertains,
yet the emptiness is always with you,
crowding out sadness, a drum
to which the pagan is alerted, glances are exchanged,
and someone, whom later no one can recall, slips out the side door?

In the bathroom there was considerable embarrassment.
One had taken off without notice, and in the sludge
that washes up on the beach are papers to be signed,
seals to be affixed. O why in this case bother a stranger, there are
enough of us to oversee the caring, the docketing; there is even
warmth on these chilly evenings of late winter, a no-season, remembering
how hot and sharp it was only a few seasons ago
when they wore their coats such-and-such a length
and cars drove by, even as they do now in certain
precincts where the roads are washed and small, trivet-shaped flowers
appear a moment and are gone, to appease the musk-god, most certainly,
and people spill out of lobbies and their greetings thicken like silt
in the runoff from a glacier and it is the standard attitudes
that are struck, there is no cry, no escape from them?

O certainly one of you must have known all this,
had it plotted for him ahead of time and said nothing: certainly
one of you runs down to the road with the news, or to get help, perhaps.

Then the idol winks and pirogues with their slanting
rows of oarsmen are seen departing backwards with undue haste.
It is time to think of spring and in pockets of not extreme despair
or under the threat of a ragged-looking but benevolent cloud, a thought
occurs: we weren't always like this, something seemed to intervene
about halfway here; at any rate a great deal of action
scrapes what we are doing into shape, for the time being. Though I am lost
I can see other points on the island, remains of picnics nearer
than one had thought, and closer still the one who comes
to resolve it all, provided you sign a document
absolving others from their eternal responsibility, swearing
that you like this light, these birds, this rattling credo
as familiar as a banging shutter, and above all, promising not
just to go about your business but to do the thing, see it drained, emptied,
a box in which four seasons will again fit
just as they did once before fire took the sky
and airplanes in their spotted plumage were seen to waver, and sink, drifting
on the wind's tune that gets in cracks here, the same
old bore, the thing already learned.

For it is indecent to last long:
one shot of you aghast in the mirror is quite enough; fog mounts
gnarled roots of the trees and one could still
stop it in time. There has to be no story, although it is
bedtime and the nursery animals strike expectant, sympathetic poses.
And then in a quiet but tense moment the crossed
identities are revealed, the rightful heir stands in the doorway.
True, it is only a picture, but someone framed and hung it;
it is apposite. And when too many moods coincide, when all windows
give on destruction, its curfew anchors us
in logic, not reprehensible anymore, not even exemplary,
though emblematic, as some other person talking in an old car would be.

POEM AT THE NEW YEAR

Once, out on the water in the clear, early nineteenth-century twilight,
you asked time to suspend its flight. If wishes could beget more than sobs
that would be my wish for you, my darling, my angel. But other
principles prevail in this glum haven, don't they? If that's what it is.

Then the wind fell of its own accord.
We went out and saw that it had actually happened.
The season stood motionless, alert. How still the drop was
on the burr I know not. I come all
packaged and serene, yet I keep losing things,

I wonder about Australia. Is it anything like Canada?
Do pigeons flutter? Is there a strangeness there, to complete
the one in me? Or must I relearn my filing system?
Can we trust others to indict us
who see us only in the evening rush hour
and never stop to think? O I was so bright about you,
my song bird, once. Now, cattails immolated
in the frozen swamp are about all I have time for.
The days are so polarized. Yet time itself is off-center.
At least that's how it feels to me.

I know it as well as all the streets in the map of my imagined
industrial city. But it has its own way of slipping past.
There was never any fullness that was going to be;
you stood in line for things, and the soiled light was
impenitent. Spiky was one adjective that came to mind,

yet for all its raised or lowered levels I approach this canal.
Its time was right in winter. There was pipe smoke
in cafés and outside the great ashen bird
streamed from lettered display-windows, and waited
a little way off. Another chance. It never became a gesture.

CENTRAL AIR

Not all the buds will open, this year or any year.
But the frame of the tree discovers this is how
what goes together gets woven together. Relief
is the thing here, the key
to all aspirations, including my own—what
do I mean, "including my own"?
Just that the shark gets tired after a few sips
of potential victims and dives off deep into
the underbelly of the sea. That signals are crossed.
That the fairies bloom in boxer shorts.

All right, but what about today,
the mystical leavening process that never occurs,
leaving us flat as crepes? How do I get
from there to here with only one side of me showing?
I can't take my pants off, that is a revolutionary
sin, akin to wiggling sideways. And this gum or
latex keeps me chained to it. There are so many floors
in this building I feel we shall never get down,
or that in the process I shall become a secret gourd
fit only for haruspication. Does that get indexed?

Anyhow, it's a downhill process.
Once that gets realized we can turn
into our parents, joining hands with them
just as the fatal drumroll is unsealed.
At that point a cat jumps out of the woodwork
to say it's all a mistake, how it'll await
your reaction as eagerly as fur takes on the aura of mist,
and goldfish turn away.

Too, some other peccadillo is missing,
which turns out to be a lucky coincidence

leading to an introduction to a memorialist
who has just turned the pages of a thrilling romance
in which a king is cuckolded and diamonds get turned into tears.
But that is all right that gets told about you;
it butters the toast, as they say in Peoria.
Yet you—here in this trattoria—
how did you get there?

Fifteen seconds ago I was no longer living.
But that's all right. You see it peps you up
to suddenly have a new book that you
are reading, happily, as print darts across pages

like larks across a field. Now, put it down.
There is someone here who says he or she knows you.

Everyone out of the house!
It was only a game of witch-tag, after all.
The spinach sky, reflected in the sea's
precise excremental tone, is what we have:
peeling posters in an old resort
announcing races on a certain July 25th.
Did we have to go? Here was more color, more options,
more reins to take, more flugel notes to be involved in.
There is nothing but business, and a businessman's
sand-colored suit, how he looked at you,
not quite sure how to take the grease-spots on your front,
yet unsure that a vacuum cleaner could remove them.
In time we just drifted apart,
and that says a lot—
says it above the drifting sound of the main, the leather breakers.
And in time we two are here.

Just as Jack had made sure that his friend Cordelia was out
and was preparing to ring the front doorbell a fleet
of blue and yellow airplanes, like frenzied butterflies,

attacked the outpost in the Falkland Islands where some
believe a secret is immured that shall save us.
But nobody ever came. Jack returned to the city where he now lectures.
As for Cordelia, it was all over in a few minutes—
she guessed that the gasp meant fiction, and proceeded
to take the necessary measures, and the sun was again wooed out
of the woods, happy to accept the throne if it
were offered, happy to retreat into senility if it were not:
it doesn't matter, it's just the way, the other way things happen,
that brings one regularly to the dentist's waiting room
with its large, appealing magazines. Meanwhile . . .

THE YOUTH'S MAGIC HORN

The gray person disputes the other's clothes-horse stature
just send us some water maybe
herding him onto the escalator for a last roll
and bitter, bitter is its taste

We don't pay contributors
just send us some water maybe
We'll talk about the new flatness
and bitter, bitter is its taste

I'll probably be sleeping with you sometime between now and next week
just send us some water maybe
I haven't made a threat that the army hasn't carried out
and bitter, bitter is its taste

Meaningless an April day hungers for its model a drawstring
just send us some water maybe
Billboards empty of change rattle along beside
and bitter, bitter is its taste

Somewhere between here and the Pacific the time got screwed up
just send us some water maybe
but my spelling, as always, is excruciatingly correct
and bitter, bitter is its taste

and I welcome intrusions like the sun
just send us some water maybe
and all around us aquifers are depleted, the heat soars,
and bitter, bitter is its taste.

First in dreams I questioned the casing of the gears the enigma presented
You're a pain in the ass my beloved
The twa corbies belched and were gone, song veiled sky that day
I have to stop in one mile

The century twitched and spewed gnomes from its folds
You're a pain in the ass my beloved
The mule-gray pilgrim was seen departing
I have to stop in one mile

I never knew the name for this brand of contumely
You're a pain in the ass my beloved
Believe me I wanted to play the shores are still beautiful
I have to stop in one mile

Here shall we sup and infest sleep for the night
You're a pain in the ass my beloved
Morning will surprise us with winds like variable coins
I have to stop in one mile

You're the truth in my cup, violet in the edge of memory
You're a pain in the ass my beloved
Retrieve me at my dying moment so shall our hearts decay
I have to stop in one mile

Remember the stone that sits beside you—
You're a pain in the ass my beloved
Sometimes they come for you and forget
I have to stop in one mile

BRUTE IMAGE

It's a question of altitude, or latitude,
Probably. I see them leaving their offices.
By seven they are turning smartly into the drive
To spend the evening with small patterns and odd,
Oblique fixtures. Authentic what? Did I say,
Or more likely did you ask is there any
Deliverance from any of this? Why yes,
One boy says, one can step for a moment
Out into the hall. Spells bring some relief
And antique shrieking into the night
That was not here before, not like this.
This is only a stand-in for the more formal,
More serious side of it. There is partial symmetry here.
Later one protests: How did we get here
This way, unable to stop communicating?
And is it all right for the children to listen,
For the weeds slanting inward, for the cold mice
Until dawn? Now every yard has its tree,
Every heart its valentine, and only we
Don't know how to occupy the tent of night
So that what must come to pass shall pass.

OF DREAMS AND DREAMING

Tell me more about that long street. Actually we're overextended;
time is running out. While still all things to all people we
are no longer swimming in the pool left by the sunrise. No, a
forest has resumed the strict narration. One puts gloves on
to ward off something. What is it? And living by a chair
so close to a thermometer no one can count is business,
that is, it can't be put aside, and coming out to your guests,
to warn them, is the recreational side we love, that, and all
things, all producers of silence that let this hay
into the tunnel and came out the far side of sleep. Really,
your life is so fascinating. I don't get it. Neither do I—
I mean I was originally the fencing instructor here.
Now my head gets buried in the flour
of reading this translucent page as a vacuum mounts,
and so off to bed. Really it's too bad, though not calculated,
and can never be—Everests of tiny snow crystals would
have to be accounted for first, and that's not likely.

Meanwhile we live in the paperweight of swirling blizzards
and little toy buses painted vermilion like the sky
when it rises up reasonably to our defense in the half-hour
after sunrise or before sunset and likes to, it likes
the idea of museums. Then so much of us is fetched away.
Often you think you can see or even smell some part of it
before it too is put away, used and put away. But then these
so recent nights would be part of the elaborate past, that old
contraption, the one we were never sure about—

It is lively still, playing to packed houses.
What must the present-day analysts think, the ones who husk it
for what that's worth, then come to play games with us

as a consequence of their own dangerous behavior.

It was night over a mountain that seemed to be there, readily
and so useful we threw ourselves on the ground dank with animal
emotions and choked-out expletives: December first! The cocksucker
hasn't been around lately we see through gaps in the dead
or is it dormant vegetation. One of us has to go the whole way now:
shall we draw straws? Don't be ridiculous but don't look
either in the direction of the walrus, the caves of the sea
hold us, though we appear to you here on this simple street
asking so little. The third time it happened I thought I was seeing
it in a new light. Then the follow-up call came. Did I want it
delivered with the sheaves of my imagination, those other ones,
and if so what would I do with these lesions marking the enchanter's
space if he is off somewhere, bold song
if ever I sang one? Though this night I shall untune
the most insistent, entrenched breaths of purpose just so I can say you
can come to me, an attack like those told of in time to
an insane purpose that is what we call history; then it will be no nearer
to a resolution, by God; I have to cry out if this mess is what is
left at my doorstep. In the future we'll
have no time for backbiting conversations like this one.
Differences will be put aside. Aye, and rainbows too, slugs
of narrative even the best of us could follow to what ends
in wild weeds, here at the wind. An' if my daughter
bring it over to you there'll be no less use for a mouse
found in your castle and turned out into blind day, the passion
some think comes at night. And we're all over you.

Suddenly it was my time. I don't know whither the watchman
vanished. He told us of the night, then vanished.
The stars are purring in the little Mississippi runoff of the
pure, bulging sky. Ours to consider, no doubt. And what if when we pay
it off, in full, it still runs toward us, too badgered to think
to mention what other tales might have been in store, only the last men

took them away. These were never seen again. My toothache is subsiding
but I won't I guess be the ultimate one, the who-by-definition-saves
what one is after, cornflower that obliges us by never appearing
in the sole instant it is wanted, but is somewhere behind that house,
no, that other one. Besides, when in doubt you can strike a match.

SEASONAL

What does the lengthening season mean,
the halo round a single note?
Blunt words projected on a screen
are what we mean, not what we wrote.

The halo round a single note
makes one look up. The careful blows
are what we mean, not what we wrote.
And what a lying writer knows

makes one look up. The careful blows
unclench a long-sought definition.
And what a lying writer knows
is pleasure, hallowed by attrition.

Unclench a long-sought definition:
what does the lengthening season mean?
Is pleasure hallowed by attrition
blunt words projected on a screen?

KAMARINSKAYA

And it was uniquely the weather, O *bombes-glacées* university!

Had they actually built something there?
It was whose turn to find out.
Tremendous lashings of cloud were pouring in, from over there, they said.
Mouths choked with news, though no news in particular,
blocked the corridor. Later aspects were discovered,
developed, and as always, they fanned out in twos and threes
or stood a little to one side to discuss whatever was being discussed.
The great moment paradigm had arrived for all of us.
Some of us reaped instant benefits. That very afternoon
we were five looking at the sea; the shore began its pitiless interrogation
and we were glad of the cleft that produced nothing and knowledge,
the freedom to wait.
                            The dentist moon hovered by the wire: *Sure,
look in thy heart and write. But don't throw foreign articles.*
And after coming down from the plateau, the heights, we are amazed
at the power of the possibilities enfolded in each thing, but above all how long
they have lasted—longer than consciousness itself. We can go on building
and the structure, the shed that joins ours, will always be there,
kind, undermining. And the strength to be indeterminate
overtakes one. There are always laws, and people to break them; that's not the point.
What is is the majestic lineage that is merely nerve endings of the air, plus spice.
It's not often we get to point to something this way,
saying:

"It must be daring or I would not have done it,
not consciously; in my sleep perhaps. And yet there are tables near mine,
close enough to overhear, and all he says is Daddy brought you,
we must make it up. Make up anything you like. Steal it
from a magazine, no one will know the difference. Use its resonance
and throw the rest away, down the steep ravine into the dump.
That way the menace is erased. And the waitress asked sweetly

if there was anything else I would be needing and I said Swell,
it's the unpinning, the unrolling of the linoleum so soon, and I
who had dwelt in realm of fancy it was I who was coming too.
There was approval all around me
and a costly lamp-base where the seconds melted and in a
gash too deep for sleep I had plotted it already, I was being told;
the light and the fences had said it. I was being rushed from leaves to tall grass
not knowing whether I had made it or whether the others had, sure only of
one piece of information in the instant harbor: the one true way
to make a book and get out alive. Surely,
the bourbon sours have stopped; now will be the declaration
of the rest of the stairway, and then we'll see.
And it's true then a locomotive may pass through like an elephant and no
one raise their eyes. The time is past, she said.
But even this wan swan song looks like news to me—
there are so many others out and getting—
and whatever happens will be red and gold like a fire engine.
Now *he* said that *she* said that he didn't know where they put it
and *she* said that *he* said that the law was over soon, that in the interim of the land
not one of us was going to cry, but many, besides we'd see
what a disaster looked like, with the moon back there and people's lack
of attention." Then he got right out and said so. Did it. But the sheriff
and his men were there. Did that mean—? But a woman read the riot act.
Now all was song, and cleaving

to the spar, that precious one, thing
that always turns up, radiant, one for the books, you must tell
them about this, really. Did that mean we had been let out?
Listen, the password is like downtown, no peace
prohibited, we can get where we want now
and can't get to but the steep ride
is safe. What do you want with me anymore? True.

ELEPHANT VISITORS

Sweet Young Thing: "Why are you all down in the mouth?"
Testy Gent: "We're all in the business of getting older,
or so it seems; we're moving on. The daytime approach
can fail you. Sit on this moment,
pause on this deck. What if the earth fell on *you*?
But the dirty salad of lies, etc., about assassination
is approaching. Something has not been found."

Here, try the gloom in *this* room.
I think you'll find it more comfortable
now that the assassins have gone away.
Or got away. Take a week and shut off the engines.
But we do have to manage to stay here in the mountains, or at least
hover, in place. There are things I still haven't told you.
What is the state flower of Nova Scotia?
On whom do we depend
when we twist downward tangled in the parachute
and the ground is coming to greet us too quickly?
That's when you could use a newspaper,
but try and find one in the prairie. I was muffled
by the elegance of it all
but now I'll take one step if only to save myself,
yes, and others. Doctors

never tell you why these four-footed quadrupeds are friends,
if only foul-weather ones. There's a lot in envelopes,
and in a hole behind the house,
but if we think we're better in this instance,
give them something they WANT. Tasseled trees.
Until which time we sign off—wait, the lotus
wants to say something: it's MADE IN JAPAN.

THE GREAT BRIDGE GAME OF LIFE

What with one thing and another they were all
too complicated. I was seen leaving.
Good grief, a frog. How funny that piece
of scaffolding flits against
yon crimson cloud, to their mutual betterment, actually.
Try saying that aloud. A nice military
mood and then where in the walk
I was mistaken and that took again.
We all fell over our numbers, if seeing
is to believing as the flat wave is on the stair.

No, scars. You forgot to pack
some. The world will live
without them and we must scurry to dream up
some other identical crisis. First it's men and
then it's me, that stayed nights
in a box, sometimes. Sometimes we were up and
sometimes we were down. It takes one of us to
reposition us and by that time danger has worn the day
down to its nub. It's best not to be
here. But if we linger after waters and cents
nothing is then too obtuse for the clime, the time
and all we travelled backward for: one good image,
the rest fenced off.

Do you think you're better for
all that clashing? The seesaw on the roof
in Zagreb disappeared, part of it.
There were no tonsils, no noodles in the paper that day.

One tries to keep oh so many
foreign things in mind but as mustard
seeps from a diary, the elegance had gone out of life.
Now there was nothing to repair.

THE DEPARTED LUSTRE

Oh I am oh so
oh so
Something is slightly wrong here,
a summer cold.

but I don't know what they're up to whether they're up to something
else because

We made it fit years ago
made it fit in
an archetypal fit

and when it didn't go on
when it took root
the ship was obliged to leave for the islands—it doesn't matter which ones.
Where it's always too hot
and the spoons are slightly bent
and someone, always some other one, saves the day
though hell-bent for the lilacs,
heedless of the volcano's warning belch
yes, and the fires are put away for that day.

Yes, like a fish I enjoy swimming lessons.
Out into the cold with us, we have mastered all that the senses
can teach us now. Only our naked intelligence
stands somewhat apart
bowed under the bowing tree.

Such speed in the letter now—
how the pen races over words, underscoring
its happiness, and all the dots and curlicues
arise under a single heaven!
It means more to me than to it

and I am lightened by the passing cry of crows
blotted like jam in the sunsets
they have here,

as the swinging touch of the earth
deepens, leads to much

and the aurora stands tall on the nimbus

of what imaginable October could be

and the mucus of mountains hardens
each day, to my surprise. Erections
surprise us in gardens.
When the fatal beauty-sleep takes over
darkness imprisons the advocates who had the key,
showed it to you, pressed it into your hand
but it was like a dream you said
it could never outlast its moment so here
we are on the ground
and a child brings you another key
whiter than the last one
to unlock pinions, positions, bookcases

where the voice can dwell unsinging

There is so much to praise,
to hate,
one is grateful for the patterns,
the obscure, plain faces,
The capital "T" in "The."

VILLANELLE

As it unfolded and took on something of the aspect
of a garden in the rain, the acclaim with which others
greeted it scattered too, evaporated. Now who
is to say when battered night comes and you look
distractedly over your shoulder, whether the owners
of that night had the right to remove any of it
in strips and mask-shaped pieces, so that by morning
nothing of it remained except crescent
accents under cups? And they were seen as truly gone,
arch-fiends of emptiness, that it stayed
to lighten awhile? What if I told you that every
aspect of the cause had been pre-ordained, from
the brokers in wind-cheaters to the tumescent
ear of corn in its shock, and that no one, not one radio,
had ever been accused of inattentiveness to the
gradual unravelling of the scene?

This would have mattered bleakly to those, the growers,
who stay behind and amid bats and laburnum devise acrostic
governors whose motives shall be colorless and whose device,
strangely scrolled across a banner, translates
easily into Urdu as: "Let's put the boys' fire out."
No, there were sad others too, but let's hear it
in the rain-bejewelled jungle gym for the copers, the
coppers-out whose ears, the brass color of tubas, flare insanely
just a little as each new podium prank thunks
into place, like a hive of bees, questioning, unsure if the date
was last year's. And if so, deliver them a warning:
mornings are timely, sure no feet drag, and yet a weariness
as of a wolf's blasts the moment into shards. We were as good
as in bed, and all
we really wanted to know was the time on the other fellow's watch.
How hard he made it, and into what twosomes the grisly smile

delivered hands, prom-dates, catches in throats, the horrible
manliness for which time is an ascending ramp crowned by moonglow
made of hundreds of cigarette ends, and the return
to town is witchy, twin scotties on a leash.

How fast the others collected! Were we to be siphoned off
as casually as last year, pinned with a string? We who
were well off until a certain day, and now, loitering, the starlet
shakes her beads in contempt: no we had not even begun to
understand where the crime is, to what
succinctness of being we are summoned if it ever goes away!
The threads, at the back, seem to match an image our fathers
dribbled, but reversed, the image is Main Street,
Titusville, and there is no other home than these
pebbles, placid and revered. There are ghosts on the trail,
too, but until we have done with hopscotch, the little girl
crawls away and twin sinkers emerge like blobs
out of the twilight, there is no point to the crash, and no end.
The house is very revealing. She said it ought to. Oh my
first fears, leaders, never
turning over, never looking back, what is it on tomorrow's
agenda? What would you have done?

A SEDENTARY EXISTENCE

Sometimes you overhear them discussing it:
the truth—that thing I thought I was telling.
What could it have been that I said?
To be more or less like other men and women
and then to not be at all—it's

like writing a book that is both beautiful and disgusting.
Because we can't do it now. Yet this space
between me and what I had to say
is inspiring. There's a freshness
to the air; the crowds on Fifth Avenue
are pertinent, and the days up ahead,
still formless, unseen.

To be more or less unravelling
one's own kindness, noting
the look on others' faces, why
that's the ticket. It is all the expression
of today, and you know how we keep an eye on

today. It left on a speeding ship.

EREBUS

I /
Tonight we are going to try a different dish
some worried savior brought us:

a vanilla-flavored tragedy
on how the market closed.

Waving from a window: that's nice.
One hears the sheeted dead
braying in a box of pencils
by that curve in the creek,

and wonders how worse things can get.
Surely there are worse things

than reading, late at night, in bed.
I would like to write a Victorian novel

of terror about a crossing-sweeper's revenge
on life, somewhat in the vein of
Lady Audley's Secret. They can can you for that

or for drawing smoke in puffs the way
it does come out of chimneys only forget

about it. The truth isn't what's wanted.
Penguin races are. Yes but you knew someone
who once knew a penguin. That doesn't matter:

put it all in your book, what you were going
to say, and wake up with a shadow,

something less meaningful on the wall.

II /

Too bad the way children
on their way to school get mislaid
and the market closes.

The honeyed wind claws at your throat.
I thought you were a fair-weather friend
but I find you here now, in tears,

begging me to give up that stratagem
I've fought a lifetime to perfect,

and I'd rather do it—for you—than bask on
the rampart of some accomplishment: always

no work, no tears, and if children
play this way, then it's all right.
I wasn't mistaken

except in dreams.

Then, Nordic champions come
to tell you how you failed
by a hair,

a breath. And you go on,
believing them. And you go on believing them

for what silver
night incurs in the pockets
of all those waiting desperately for a sequel.

But it comes round
to this: what is comic is no longer

fatuous, and you're the first to learn about it and can keep silent about it and make a killing. In the meantime your door is white as snow.

THE OLD COMPLEX

As structures go, it wasn't such a bad one,
and it filled the space before the eye
with loving, sinister patches. A modest
eyesore. It reduced them to a sort of paste
wherein each finds his account, goes off
to live among the shore's bashed-in hulks.

Of course you have to actually take the medicine.
For it to work, I mean. Spending much time upstairs
now, I can regulate the solitude,
the rugged blade of anger, note
the occasional black steed. Evening warbles away.

You are free to go now, to go free.
Still, it would help if you'd stay one more day.
I press her hand, strange thing.

WHERE WE WENT FOR LUNCH

I /
The boss made it official.
Then a cherub came out and sassed us.
"Why do you listen to all this *chamber music?*
Why don't you ever listen to church music?"

Indeed, I thought I had always done so,
but now I had other things to worry about.
"Other things to worry about"—he keeps repeating that phrase
as though it were an escutcheon on a portcullis.
What manner of ridicule is this? Of course
there's nothing to worry about, except your response,
which is precisely what dissolves in music—you know the kind,
that keeps coming round again, like a customer
to a neighborhood bar, and some good exchanges
take place between a couple of fiddles, who then decide to walk home together.

Shit, if this were New York . . .
In the next episode he sees me with the eyes of a cat.
"You remembered . . . to bring . . . the gold stuff?"
Oh sure, but I'm not a catalog, nor
what's wanted here. I'm a Belgian
with lots of Belgian things to think about
such as newspapers and old shoes stuffed with same—say I think
I'll get out of here too. I don't know about you. This
cement sidewalk looks pretty steep to me, though it's broad . . .
(Hah, that part always fools them.) I say,
what if we took a turn through the thicket down there—
might clear our eyes out, *if you know what I mean.*

I do. But I keep returning to what is in dreams
for me, not certain I'm correct, that this place is suitable.
I think I'll lie on the shore, fighting with the sand,

for a little, if you don't mind. And then one of those parrots—
we might see one, eh? Oh he thinks he's Crusoe now.
So much for the general populace's idea of loneliness—
I thought they'd abandoned it years ago, but they still
like to keep up the pretense. "You think *you're* alone?"
No, I never said that, you are deliberately twisting my words,
but twist them you must, if you think you must.
Right now I'd like a long cool twist of something.

Sure, she goes out with *some* men.
But that don't mean you . . . Oh, hell,
there I go trying to make something of something
again. Time to pull in one's horns, me buckoes, if you
catch my drift. And if we don't? Then it will catch you, sure as
wavelets nibble little by little at the sandbar
they have no idea of covering completely in fewer minutes
than it takes to play an old 78 r.p.m. record, say,
make it nice this time, how about Dvorak's *Humoreske?*
I was just going to ask you about that word. They don't
make 'em any more. We don't have any in stock.
We are about a shout.

Why, when it comes time to saunter, why
we'll do that too. I was first desk at the Vienna *Musikverein.*
It was during the second Viennese school. Why do poets like to eat?
Why, you do something, you want people to know about it, it's as
simple as that, at least it seems so to me, but
I could be wrong, I have been in the past, and about more things
than you, Horatio. By the way, how's that bridge coming along?

II /
When we sleep we see sweet things
and are wiser next day.
I forgot to play
yesterday. I'm all stiff today.

III /

Seriously, what were we made to talk about? Just casters on a floor, that always leave something of a mark nevertheless. I will have to have my will read to you. That's as close to a tease as we ever get. This elevator just dropped seven floors and no one knew anything about it. Nobody thought they were going to die. Can you stand stupid people? Yes, me too, there's something so, well, *stupid* about them, they're like earthworms coming through a mound of dirt, you just have to love them. They're the ones with the passion. Now, there's something I'd like to have. Many's the time I've been chided for my presumed lack of it, and rightly too. Oh I know what I'd do if I had some, who I'd go over and see first. But if you can't have it you can't get it. That's where this thing called "intelligence" comes in. See, there's more to it than you thought—than *I* thought. If we can find our intelligence, and everybody has some, we can use it to make little stick figures out of Plasticine whose elbows we can bend, and then there is no expression more touching, my God I'm getting all crazy-eyed just thinking about it. We can make our own little race, and they have cars to fit. But I'm getting ahead of myself, my story, really. But I've told it to you. We can just look at each other and blink. Or not. We can just sleep together.

And when I was having lunch
I heard this voice singing
about the breath of other planets blowing.
I mean, who needs to be reminded?
I am at your doorstep after all,
sliding down the door, I pick up the knocker and replace it softly.
There seems nowhere to go,
nothing to do.

I can ask you out on some pretext,
only don't be lonely,
see?
There are enough unhappy people in this gyre.
But I was never one of them and now you will be too.

AS OFT IT CHANCETH

You had but to look at a mound or nut
after the invention of perspective for it to become a rut.
Everybody was seeing and doing it.
That is why some few choose disorder
as scenery befitting the positive melancholy of their stance,
which means to get things done in a climate of awkwardness.
The perfidious sky tore past them,
its ribbons streaming revolt, and soon,
not right away, it would be time to go down to the street
to inhabit that walking shell of you
that by this time is all either of us knows of the other,
but it *is* something.

Pick up your room.
Your visitor is coming up the walk,
the door-chime sounds. Now if only in a second I could invent
the leagues of prosperous businessmen I mean to have commerce with; but no,
it is allegory still. The house on the hill,
the bramble bush, the neighbor, disappearing
along that appropriate perspective.
You believed it if it was convenient; otherwise
you may have believed it anyway, and it was all
shaken out, like clothes.

But in the room the guardians of same will have it
their way. And though this will never cause the temperature to change,
there are still others filling up the anteroom
with the breath of fog, with wishes not voiced
for a while, until it becomes obnoxious and incinerating not to
have them, in their way, as they crest down
on us. Anybody could've thought it up, but, funny,
no one ever did until that elaborate hour
wherein we go on seeing, and our order is taken.

RETABLO

After it had jiggled down it came out OK.
Drugstores sold it. You to whom this awful mission has been
entrusted are barred, of course, from commenting
while it is held up in the courts
and none of your family or lawyers can, either,
which is unfortunate at a time
when such a lot depends on being supple and risky, the way
you always were, of course,
except that now it isn't quite enough, is it,
as was the case on certain days
gray and blustery, but otherwise quite undistinguished, quite
unmemorable. You had to choose.
Did I forget to mention that? It came with the package
and had to be peeled off and mailed back, but even that
foretaste of doom didn't rate a footnote, while other, less
notable and possibly less objectionable aspects dropped
out of the stone forehead, leaving it black,
something to be pitied, almost.

So much more came untied during the swinging
of the bell ropes and of course the maddening pandemonium of the bells
themselves—they get right inside your head—
that someone would invariably stop to ask, Hey what is this
redemption stuff anyway, all this talk about bonds and escrow—
wasn't it supposed to be on a more spiritual shelf
where presences of sages nod and fall on each other,
falling asleep all over each other,
and at noon the terriers run and die as though these
treehouses were meant for someone else who would fit them out
differently, all spare and nautical? Captain, you've got to tell me,
what is this insane voyage about? I haven't even bought a ticket
and besides am on dry land heading back to see my aunts and cousin, aw,
have a heart will you? And these garbage-flecked

shoals beyond the barrier reef, you can't tell me those orange-
haired floozies are sirens! Hell, I can hear 'em.
And *I'm* going nowhere, that's for damn sure, as I know you
know in this vacuum you label interest in other people's lives,
in seeing how they accomplish what they set out to do.

Probably the rain never got loose
for all you know, but it did, it was like cellophane noodles escaping
from a slashed envelope. I had a transparent raincoat to prove it,
but it wasn't enough, that wasn't enough, nothing was enough to be quiet
in the little schoolhouse, but it *was* enough to know the last
class was over many seasons ago. There was something learned once but
it had drained out through a ring of rust in the middle of the floor,
and besides the desk-captains never kept such good time
any more, but of course there was less to know in those days:
only a few harness-bells, and a heap of dust and straw.
Which reminds me: why are you shivering under that horse-blanket
when there's so much to be done by way of filing
the last perennials, each in its separate slipcase, and of not letting Jack get away.

He's got more to do; there's more to be done
than any of us ever dreamed of, whole pockets and mountains
of it, let into the side of a cloud hill.
Then the worrying starts, a fresh leak of pain
squirts through the tape and soon the bandage is loosened,
useless in the grass where I was standing all along, a picture
to myself. So the long rain waves drain;
there's a sense of compactness, or even nothing, though all the ships
have returned from Iceland, with stars, and with the scarves that sent them there.

A MOURNING FORBIDDING VALEDICTION

And who, when all is said and done,
Cares for thee like me? I know. *Thy* name
Is known to me, and if thou sufferest like a squall
That sirens rend, I'll be confident and of the other
Persuasion. Perfume that drenches like a pall
Is the old scent, and dear, true; its fame
Waxeth with the sun
And is not like, moreover, a lost brother.

When glory's steed pawed the ground,
Frozen and flinty the hour, yet for some
It was command out of the deepest basin, and who shall say
Which recombinant molecules have memorized the next rote
And when the reciters have fall'n, on a day
Stuck in time's craw, that merriment is a crumb
Unfit for sharing, only a sound
Like itself, endless fishy smell or zygote.

Nothing's here; the year
Is ripe, and frozen, all about me stand
Censors—veiled, tumescent husks who at the last
Come clean in the moulting of the season, and make no bones
About their city of origin. Them too, held fast
In Memory's drizzle, the Place St. Ferdinand
Negates, and surrounding highrises, mere
Chaff, or the power which breeds stones

And shall have much to say, come night-
Fall, and all around us awful blisters concur
In melting trusses, stalk the errant ptarmigan
Or deed no entry to fools and nimble savants beyond the moat
That weeps for times when the green cardigan
Of duckweed shrouded it, and, all exemplary, her

Nose protruded beyond the outline of the bight
Some saw beyond, and her raincoat.

To scrape the habit from our stand of being, and, once
It's accomplished, rescue it from shyness, out of a burrow
Of pleasure up toward greater mounds of pleasure, is to a name
What places are, and so be it
If trace elements are added and rules from the game
Subtracted little by little. Ergo,
Someone's won it. Dunce
Am I? So's your old man, you stupid shit.

Gallons and gallons of water slid over the weir
But since it was night, no one knew or cared. The owl,
For all his feathers, was a-cold. Peace lay in sections
On the raised edge of a circus ring, where sawdust
Conjures belly's emptiness and the recent elections
Are commented. Men prowl
Beside the recently abandoned pier
Sprung from any concept, from reckonings, crust

Of someone else's negligence, our cognizance.
O skate too far away, or else backpack, backtrack
Into the hay of an argument dimly seen, unscathed
Like time. The more marbles to our monument
The more the future won't be any less real to us, enswathed
In Hyperborean conundrums—that's as may be. To bushwhack
From here to Petaluma, then chance
Failed irrigation canals, faults, is my soul's sole integument.

I FOUND THEIR ADVICE

When you hear the language
(not the spirit of the language) it unfolds like a shelf
just to be equal with the level you have risen to.
A change takes place. No longer are steel leviathans erected
at points of entry to the city. The clouds have come down
to be a part of what they and we so long dreaded.

And we who cling in wonderment to a sheer surface
like chains of bubbles, we who talk and lecture,
know that it is half-past five, that what we were learning
has begun.

Who thought we weren't learning because we hadn't stopped learning,
know all learning is going. In the silence, the dear gray
crevices are scrutable as ever. But knowing
time as a blur comforts us, seals us
from inherited light, too fast and unsorted: who
knows what organic matter is contained there,
what difference to the environment?

The last fires are banked, the strip-search is less precise.
Now they just ask you what you're doing here,
or were doing here; it's not a ceremonial
but it doesn't jostle. The garden, the atrium are included
I'm afraid in the voice of praise, and the sleeping vines
machined for this feeling that has to leave:
willful, a chance for us.

FRENCH OPERA

Hi. I'm Bob.
The long flight is over
and they have returned to the places
where they live in the ground.

The beloved past
is near, cautiously optimistic:
I've laid so much drawing over
the empty, original square, that it
almost ties figure
to ground, plot to decaying
character, last year with next.

I'm like a keeper of drawings:
they're fragile, lonely sometimes,
like best friends erected on the dark lace
of the sometime sonatas. Only let me not
checker my face with the derring-do of
having once been somewhere, of
having been brought down from the mountains
to testify in court, and gone back up again,
senseless, the stenographer reminds
us. We're trying to adhere
to it, to give you some money to tell her
you're here. In the responsory we could make
it go somewhere, round and round
the track if you wish, but do we
know where they teach? Do they sing?

In French opera, Charpentier's *Julien*,
for example, the problem is always the listener's:
trying to make sense of it all and feel sorry
for the characters and *still* keep faith

in ourselves and what others are doing, industriously,
nay, zealously, and the payoff
is always
in the next yard.

Still, no building collapses.
Reinforcements are on the way.
There is a whole lot of colored
imagery to sort out and sift away,
being careful not to get any of it
on one's clothes. There are forklifts
and fedoras. In short this *is* that
old chapel scene you once wanted to know
about, except that moving sands cover
the boards then as always.
You might wish to shift in your chair.

.

A STIFLED NOTATION

No one ever oversleeps
until the time you are to improve your life, and then
what's one superstition more or less?
The lives, I guess. And it's best to be early
about things, not drink too much,
lest the pattern be seen in its undoing.
The judges march backward up the steps.

Well, you've solved this week's problem,
but the wind is wailing a little too enthusiastically
as the garden takes up the fugue at a point
where it's impossible to be lonesome and valid anymore.
The fishes swim, birds plod fustily
with heaven-dividing cries, until the whole world seems soaked
in the boredom of that sorrow you were promised,
but also
crazy with love and self-deception. Sometimes a charcoal sketch
of a refrigerator is supposed to be the edge.
How long you had no aim
for no other stream.

HAUNTED STANZAS

It has been raining on and off for a week now:
drip, drip. Already we are beginning to feel the effects of this,
as life slides insensibly onward. In one corner
a harpsichord is shelling peas. Watch out for rowboats!

When the new series of etudes was published it
caused quite a stir in the musical world.
Darkness was more perfect. Happiness no longer
was a thing to hold on to, but became a great curve,
listening instead. We don't know what pressures
you to behave as we do. We only do it out
of fear and love, meddling like
guardian angels with what does in fact concern us
a little.

Unbattered the storm plays, like a lion cub,
the bolts tremendous, and the basement is still coming apart.
I am less than enthused though a cautious display of differentiated
levels would be the appropriate note here. The thing done,
and the apron that came after.

I am not prepared to give up my life for a few drawings.
Nevertheless I want reassurance, as if this were the Mesozoic era and
people saw themselves differently as so much meat and whiskers.
I'm not sure I wouldn't have been enchanted
to have those advantages and see how women live when they're away
from men and don't have to think about it.

So the carpenter makes a list of
whatever *might* be needed and the ritual
gains in transparency from that.

Even the little piles of dust in the schoolyard had their say
and thought differently about it only they came to be in the end
what navigators had never asked for: the whole planisphere
pressed into one's hand like currants.

Who praises rigor?
The ones who have less to lose. Who live
in harm's way and poetry is as a vice to them. Never
mind, it is more meaningful that the settlers were unwearied,
as, given our best days, we all are. So I feel connected,
the car slithers forward, meanwhile

let me lick your shirt. I have an honest proposition to make
to you, one that I hope you'll find rewarding: turn
your back so as not to see the parade of prisoners escaping.
It'll do them good and it'll do you good. You have it in your power
to offer proof of the equations amid the alembics of the tower
where the gas flares and your nerves buzz. Well?

Shouldn't you be off and running? Until another day, then.
And he saddles his horse, which he called "Old Paint" (never
knew why, except that its rough exterior was somewhat suggestive of old paint)
and that was it. But I want to pray for you, whole
afternoons-worth, I do. But sometimes the sledge is honest. It bears us away.

LIVELONG DAYS

Feather in your cap? Not from heeding
the half-lit messages of other writers
you cherish and would like to forget.
I sat at my desk; the storm was brewing
on an April morning. The sun still shone
and the bud had blasted. There were shadows on the ground.
Yet I sat, not doing, not worrying whether we're living in it right.
And when her younger sister found out who I was,
why, that would take precedence. Certainly
we'd all be here a while longer
that would mean time to find out,
to test the fiddle's scrolled-up tensions
in case everything came out all right.

Those were the days for living in a sack,
a loose one for answering the door in.
The neighbors kept you up all night
with whispering and indecisions. It was time to
look into "Aunt Agatha's Tried and True Recipes" just to see
who was mulling it and if they could
somehow get back to you once the joint was cold.
Alas, these spoke only in terms appropriate to the occasion,
too much so, in fact. Where was the residue
of calm fear, the notices
to convene with the lawn chairs, that prompted inspection of other
recent ordinances? And the doormat wiggled like a ghost
in the draft under the door but there was quite a lot to be said
and none willing to go down, slog down if need be, the painted stair
whose ends were invisible
in this tide of sick summer light
wherever feet chose to take one, here
among the weeds and provisions, there in the rue,
and make chaff of all we built, all we had constructed against.

That is a way of being, it said. All right,
I won't argue, but show me the increment, fine as lint,
apparently, that tips it, festoons
a tree in the room, and finally delivers the book
to a publisher just as the door is closing. I won't envy it.
If I had the wings of an angel something, or everything,
would be slightly different, and you'd see: it would
come out in play. The differences that make us inexact now would
chase us into learning from that space, that pure longing
for the pauses just past, multiplying like mythologies, apples.

QUARTET

Always

because I saw the most beautiful
name go down ahead of mine

I'm banished to an asteroid
perfect meld of soppy common sense
with somewhere a loose connection

only don't make me think it
always
I'm figuring out what went just before
with that which comes too late:

invitation to a pool party
where the hors-d'oeuvres are free
as well as the first drink but not
the later ones
this was pretty late in the season

for me I told a tired invisible guest
but one must invade new premises
scout new locations
from time to time I said he seemed
to agree

that my date hadn't been seen in some time
oh well I was trying to lose her suppose
we go upstairs and just have a look round
flash bulbs popping
I said
well anyway as it is baked so shall it endure

and the co-ordinated midriffs be here
at 10:30 sharp no one moves
before every hand is on stage I
think I know what that meant he said
there'd be no more coffee and doughnuts
before this smooth introduction I believe I'm
one of your friends of course he said make room for Miss Scott

I suppose it's idle of me to worry
how other people will take the cold
it belongs to each of us like a blanket
and like fear doesn't go away
though it does go away in the evening
and return in the morning
and each of us deals with it
like bowels or bladder like

it or not I said we is each
a machine for milling or sorting whatever
gets digested or eliminated there's no
planning to stop for a while
taking a brief vacation
taking in some theater or old film
it's useless because bad
we pronounced ourselves part of the
joint agreement

and indeed I just meant to come back for a moment
to make sure I hadn't left anything behind
and lo and behold I am the central protagonist
in this cabana and all that was
going to be hid from me is hid
and everything looks quite normal
and so I shall approve the document
there's no earthly reason not to

is there
I said and he said no it's all past in the weather

and no matter what private associations are
set in motion by this train of thought no
change can ever be the result
I saw where he was leading
and it was centuries before I could disentangle
my sense of what I thought was right from the legal
obligation to bind everything into a sheaf
to recognize myself on your mirror
when we both returned to the dark pond
agreeing it best to nourish the affection
with toasts and witty consolation

rather than undertake a new epic
that might get bogged down in production
anything rather than those covered wagons
converging on a new day and he said I'm with you
I can't understand what the cue cards
mean about it snowing outside the sanitarium
solarium and is it true I am to spend my entire life meddling
with someone else's desires and then piecing
everything together just before it all blows up and I can
say yes once I had the meaning of it it was pretty good
and now all can see the meaning in it and I have forgotten
it all but it all still seems pretty good I guess he said

And now I cannot remember how I would have had it. It is not a conduit (confluence?) but a place. The place, of movement and an order. The place of old order. But the tail end of the movement is new. Driving us to say what we are thinking. It is so much like a beach after all, where you stand and think of going no further. And it is good when you get to no further. It is like a reason that picks you up and places you where you always wanted to be. This far. It is fair to be crossing, to have crossed. Then there is no promise in the other. Here it is. Steel and air, a mottled presence, small panacea and lucky for us. And then it got very cool.

Everyone seemed pleased, even the then-invisible statisticians
who brought us to this pass. My barometer is working well;
a drop of milk in the scudding blue thinks so.
Maybe if I were shorter
the sky would stand up to greet me contemptuously
in that endearing way it sometimes has. My train is being flagged down.

Surely it's time to go where they want us to go.
I was never big on reading
though I enjoyed singing when I knew the words
which wasn't that often. And you, you sang with me
in the evenings for a while, and Minnie and Joe the goat joined in.

It was as impossible to enjoy the unseemliness of that present
as it was not to forget it, to cover it with showers
once spring had come. Once spring had come
the gigantic tail of a horse projected beyond the barn door.
The tail, I mean the tale, was beginning for us again
in ways too complicated to scrutinize, but we did come up with a set of questions.
Then the interviewer said that was all for that day.
The vice-president looked tired.

Back in my shack at low tide
I rehearsed the speech I would never have occasion to deliver.
Once I put pebbles in my mouth
though it lent no conviction to the list of wildflowers I was annotating.
I would say that on the whole it has been a good experience,
but I would also say that everything has been a good experience.
I touched needles, and learned how they were sharp.
Later I became a sharp dresser
having mastered the art of mix and match.
I think I'm going home now, to tea, it's sleepy:
just say maybe sir, ask the right gent

about it, he always gets it right
and then we're on the right track, which is always a relief,

isn't it? *But I have something to tell you.*
It was wrong of you to play this far, first; and when you had finished
you should not have raised your eyes to the sea that blinded us
through the open doors, even as you thought you had married it
and were obliged to. Or something. At this rate none of us will get our
sponge in time, while the river overflows with fish.
Be careful of that puddle.
If they knew we had indulged each other—but what earthly
use does anything have? Why are we here? I'll tell you:
it's so the little naked man can run out into the grass
that towers over him, sprayed with dewdrops,
to massacre the cold
and master the changed legions
whose breath never hurt
anything, but you are loved and it's your responsibility.

JUST WEDNESDAY

So it likes light and likes
to be teased about it—please
don't take me literally. That winter light
should be upon us soon in all its splendor—
I can see it now—and the likes of the haves
shall mingle with the have-nots, to some point
this time, we all hope, and the pride encoded
in the selection process that made us what we are,
that made our great religions fit us,
will be deployed, a map-like fan so you can
actually sit down

and find us where we came from. True, some
at first claimed they recognized it and later
admitted they didn't, as though the slow rise
of history were just some tune. That didn't prevent others
from really finishing the job, and in the process
turning up points of gold that are we say these
things we shall have, now. And the jolly
carpentered tune merely played along with all that
as an obbligato, but on a day
took up residence in its own strength.
A weary sense of triumph ensued but it was the reality
of creation. There were no two ways.

And so one emerged scalded with the apprehension of this,
that this was what it was like. You gave me a penny, I
gave you two copies of the same word that were to fit
you like rubber ears. Is it my fault if in the dust
of the sensation something got knowingly underscored, defaced,
a shame to all the nation?
After all, it suited when you set out dressed
in plum and Mama was to meet us at the midpoint

of the journey but she got taken away and an old
dressmaker's dummy draped in soiled lace was substituted
for the intricate knowledge at this juncture.
The grass grew looser but closer together,
the flowers husky and fierce as trees. On the spiffy
ground no wagers were taken and a few minutes'
absence is the bee's knees. It behooves

you to depart if the moon is cowled.
That homeless blanket you gave up—
you should have sent them both years ago. A few
cronies still gather there where the shore
was explained and now the waves
explain it with renewed mastery and suds. Almost
time for the watchman to tell it to the lamplighter
and I'll be switched, after all these years.

IN MY WAY / ON MY WAY

Pardon my appearance. I am old now,
though someday I shall be young again. Not, it's true, in the near future.
Yet one cherishes a hope
of being young before today's children are young grandparents,
before the gipsy camp of today has picked up and moved
into the invisible night, that sees,
and sees on and on like a ritual conscience
that bathes us, from whose dense curves we know
we shall never escape. We like it here as the trial begins,
the warming trend, more air, even the malicious smile in the prefecture garden—
would we like it as much *there?* No, for we only like what we already
know, what is familiar. Anything different
is to be our ruin, as who stands
on pillars and pediments of the city,
judging us mournfully, from whose cresting gaze is no
turning away, only peering back into the blackness of the pit of water of night.

Once I tried to wriggle free of the loose skein of people's suggestions
chirping my name. One can do that if one is rich. But for others a bad
supposition comes of it, there is more death and pain at the end,
so that one is better off out of the house, sleeping in the open
where chiggers infest the lilacs, and a sullen toad sits,
steeped in self-contemplation. By glory I had
better know before too long what the verdict is. As I said I was changing
to more comfortable clothing when the alarm bell sounded.
Which is why I am you, why we too
never quite seem to escape each other's shadow.
Perhaps drinking has something to do with it
and the colored disc of a beach umbrella, put up long ago against the sun.

Yet even where things go wrong there is more
drumming, more clatter than seems normal. There is a remnant of energy
no one can account for, and though I try

to despise my own ways along with others, I can't help placing
things in the proper light. I am to exult
in the stacks of cloud banks, each silently yearning
for the upper ether and curving its back, and in the way all things
seem to have of shaping up before the deaf man comes.
O in a way it is spiritual to be out from under these
dead packages of the air that only inhibit
further learning and borders, as though these too came to see the sea
and having done so, returned
to selfish buildings enclosed by walls. Their conceit
was never again to be quite as apt as that time that is remembered
but no more, on a quilted sea of pylons and terminal anxiety
far from the rich robe, imagined and unimagined, as far as the pole
is from us. As around the pond, several rods away, the liquid
performance starts and repeats, endlessly.
We live now in *that* dust
but no one shakes it, no finish is yet prized, prized and forgotten.

As when we bumble, maintaining steadfastly that there is no life in the truth of us,
no bearings in the grass, and who cares anyway, why the salt
on his fingertip is life enough for us under the present circumstances,
something always focuses attention on all we have done since school,
how we were naked, and fell, and those
coming up behind dutifully picked us up and presented us as evidence
and the court in a major shift decided to hear the arguments
and all was sadness, it was decreed, for a while,
till pregnant pauses were abandoned, and miniskirts returned, and with them
a longing for a future of fashionable choices,
dotted earthworks in the comforting desert,
various fruits to assuage thirst
and the almost maniacal voice of your leader
reminding us of practical solutions so out of date they were all but forgotten.

Far from fear of crowds stumbling,
what ought to incite you is a new hunger for all the angles of whatever
day this is, placed against the sandstone of undoubted

approval from many different quarters.

True, all that we hurled

returns to visit, and true too that the bayoneted

clock recovers, that composure is a gift

that sometimes the gods bestow, and sometimes not; their reasons in the one

as in the other case remaining inscrutable even to apple-

scented mornings where the light seems newly washed, the gnarled trees in the prime

of youth, and the little house more sensible than ever before

as a boat passes, acquiescing to

the open, the shore, the listless waves that distract us

out of prurience and melancholy, every time. Yet something waits.

I can hear the toad crooning. It's almost time for intermission.

The guest register awaits signing. It's another, someone's, voyage.

NO GOOD AT NAMES

We've been out here long enough.
The past recedes like an exaggeratedly long shadow
into what is prescient, and new—
what I originally came to do research on.
I have my notes, thank you. The train is waiting
in the little enclosed yard. My only duty
now is to thank all those who put up with me
and trusted me so long. It must have seemed
like a long process. My thanks are due, too,
to others with whom I never came in contact,
who may not have been alive, but
somehow we were in apposition, and as my pen
strikes out on its own, it is chiefly those others
I wish to remember. In a word, *merci*.

And at random stages of the journey he sees
what we were meant to see: underwear on a clothesline,
flying leaves, patches of dirty snow. It's true no one
ever tests you on these things, that nothing would have been different
if you hadn't seen them all, yet by emerging
they have become part of the picture, so vast and energetic
it gets seen by nobody. Later, in the station,
you greet a small group of close and not-so-close friends,
sparring about would the bargain have been different
if it had happened in something resembling a time-frame,
or a landscape, even a landscape one has only heard about.
And you show each other your clothes, smiling shyly,
and talk about the after-effects of the medication
everyone's taking these days, and it seems to have made
a difference, brought out the leaves in the public squares.

Great travel writing has to be manufactured this way
for the desert's glitter to sink back into something tractable

and frozen antennae to balk at the day's closing prices.
A moment of horrible witchcraft isn't too much to be swallowed
for the land to become whole, and people wise
in the way that suits them.

FILM NOIR

Just the washing of the floors
under him was cause for hope. If there was a flaw
in something precious, it meant one or more persons
had been inducted already. When they heard about it
it would come to seem as though the rich background
was you, your space. It lent you
a furious dignity that you breezed right through.
No more apples on the dashboard,
this is cheating the real thing, earnest
with life and self-assurance. And when you died
they remembered you chiefly. It was two
lights on a rowboat, a half-mile off shore
as the evening breeze drew nigh, cementing relationships.
And it seemed as though they always heard you, loud you,
that otherwise nobody remembered except conveniently.

When the inevitable abrupt change arrived
I looked to you for reflected confirmation of what
was happening to me, and unfortunately got it.
The afternoon windows released their secrets in a flood
as though no one had ever had any. In the downpour
distinct noses and adam's-apples could be determined
in a mounting hush of congratulation soon to be
shattered by a train's ear-piercing whistle:
the doors slid shut, there was nothing to do except wait
for another train, yet this one still stayed at the platform.
Too bad suicide is discouraged
in certain modern climates and situations; it makes
for such a neat ending; nevertheless we will brush on,
clinging to separate ideas as though they made a pattern.
And all shall be insulted

at the end where the going gets sticky
beyond any apology, beyond dried beans and casual sex, beyond even
the neighbor's girl in a schoolyard, half a century ago
when things still seemed pretty modern
and underlying motives were the same
though not the dark, intricate working out of them.
Say we just landed, like strangers in a hole:
what manner of manners is to be cut out of us, what sails
trimmed for the descent
into the matter of the sun.
Are Americans sexier, she breathed, or what is it
that gives their nudes a subliminal variation
on this often rehearsed enterprise, until we can see
into it, arranging differences? And that moan
you heard was just idle gossip, someone running around
to instruct the clerks of our compassion
in rules, rhetoric or some other tell-tale destiny
if we are about to get it right again.

But on the curb of the residential street
where wind thrives and the locals
shrug off any connection to the scenery, back where it was bad,
the same dichotomy obtains. We and they.
It's not much more simple than that.
And as I approach the master switch
for instructions, there are little smiles of recognition
everywhere, in the curdled clouds, on the reluctant shore,
to tell us it's safe to go home.

I hope they can come.
They can sleep under my bed.

IN VAIN, THEREFORE

the jetsam sighs,
flooding the front hall,
with the fragile violence etched
on the captain's forehead:

some got off at the next-to-last stop;
others, less fortunate
were lost on the trail,
pines and mist carrying over
until the exit wicket

displaced all thoughts of a former, human time.
We, it was reasoned,
led lewd lives, belong with the bears.

A very few carry enough energy to
create a kinetic bonding arrangement.
These are the so-called sad ones
eating alone in restaurants,
drying their hair . . .

The dandelions are dead and the mud
of summer. They
tell of roasted meats, be oblivion
but a decade away
and the waterfall, unused,
is ruined, it is ruined, is not to stand.

THE BEER DRINKERS

Think of it as something that is happening
or something that is merely in the way, unnamed
until we call a meeting, go over it, eat it.
And then of course so much more of it is found
than was really necessary. Look at this season.
Trees are shiny, trapped in prisms. Umbrellas
are a new, raw color. The temperature's
not what it's supposed to be yet. Look. Enjoy.
Your house comes clattering down around you
like beads from a string. That's
nice. Each has its strength, its subliminal magic
and knows just how to keep out of the way
until the time for its expression is scratched
into the rude stone. How it will be forever.

You couldn't do that young. Now,
you set about what is going, and already
find it refreshed. And what of the new year?
It had an air of finality to it when last seen
but weathers wash so many of what we are, it
seems lame at last, then crowded into the omnibus
with all the fates, and furies, and us
of course, and the folks from home. How we
managed it yet again is a tale
for the newspapers by now, but how
the wariness of the telling could so
stock a nursery is something that continues
to baffle authorities. And all the colors
put up for sale, were they meant to
go by us two, and what is the change.

They have this tremendous power
in their doing, these Americans, and next you

know a coin extracted from a pouch
will be seen to be the real truth serum,
only you cannot get away just now
and in the autumn the roads freeze over.
And then of course he added distance
and rightness to them, and they came
apart amazed, and he was in someone else's camp
but could write to you. And you were embarrassed
in a bathrobe and it shut them all up.
He was only dying to air these anemones as a truth
and the truth shot all over him
and he came, and of course that one fact annihilated him.
Time for toasts now, darling? I think
rather, and hope I shall see him long
one of these evenings before the new snow starts.

THAT YOU TELL

The cannons waved summer goodbye
and the long arcs of breathing took up where they left off:
speechless. An old jalopy with wobbly wheels was seen to limp
into an abandoned filling station. Autumn sticks
in your throat; you must have a reason for doing anything now,
such as looking in a place you were sure
they weren't. Then you find something. Money jingles,
brightness is for a second. Then the cars, crows and cows walk away.

In sixteen years it hadn't been like this ... this
symphonic stretch. How room had been created
before the notion of what was to go in it actually existed,
and yet by becoming, it did. And already had a history.
You, you were in it too. It started to curl back on us
like a sheet at night, and the choices were somehow limited,
the instructions far from complete. You must go down
to the shore of the steeply flowing river and assuage
whatever they call gods there. Then the reflected shimmer waxes bright
again. This is the prologue. The irises are dark
and prudent, and I like my male-pattern baldness. Far at sea
porpoises and businessmen are asleep
taking us farther than can be imagined, to the floor above.

I knelt and listened. There was nothing unusual,
no appearance of impropriety. Meals were prepared again,
the summer's sheaf raided, rains drowned the meadows pell-mell
under the eyes of peasants. Is what I'm being singled
out for, to tell of this, while the main population
of truants escapes over nearby hills? If so, so be it:
I've taken my stand and am pretty much prepared
to let it wear me out. Nor does the crucible of what we said
out of turn return to urge a new complacency, quiet
between the paws of the sphinx, nor does anything electrical have to interfere.

I know the air itself is noxious. I must breathe it
for those who can't; only let the nodes be protected from themselves
that in some joyous valley, far from here, picnicking
can occur under the vines, and the
tiniest constituents be sorted and drained, and approved.

The opposition has its way
always. See that neon fence? It spells out too much common sense,
which is a good thing, in the sense that memory is voided.
Afterwards, the monoliths grow untended;
something strange and seedy in the sky though centralization
has finally been realized after how many decades
of struggle and one may live
in these little homes, with their gardens, and all
be complete for a few more years. But I think the stealth
is a parasite hidden in it somewhere, that soon
other towns and banks discourage newcomers and there is a shortage
of the most vital commodities and even time
has almost run short. Now, tell it to your teachers,
kids, how well off we were and what you were going to write
in your essay about the conversion. What is vast is also hollow,
ragged with age, riddled with false modesty and complaints
from divers sources, including death. It seems
the truth was about something else, various and vicious, or it was
these very elements but mostly
a protracted span. And when it was over, that was the truth:
a nest of eggs still hidden, the false flight of a bird.

A HOLE IN YOUR SOCK

A man walks at a city
as though veering off somewhere.
They extend arms, touch hands.
This is how it is done, every day.

My phone is tapped.
I wish to call the police.
Not, not obviously, part of the
"proceedings,"
the message takes control smoothly.

We contemplate the shells of crustaceans
long dead, waiting for the Bronze Age to end.
We go farther, fare worse.
And they gave us our little raincoat back.

Then the government gets into the act
and the others crowd in and out.
That was something, sainthood
of a sort. You have to take it.

They simply ... die. And that's it.
When we come back
in fortuitous weather
the charm has multiplied beyond the sky,

is ever so contemporary,
as an ingredient should be.
The class marshals, boring thespians
have walked on. A teardrop
stands in the middle air.

This future does us good.

AND SOCIALIZING

Back from his breakfast, thirty-five years ago,
he stumbles, finds in the sun a nod that's new.
Which is not to say we are any better off than a second ago.
These days, by turns solemn and skittish, our days,
belong to someone who once was here. More we cannot say.

Yet a vague pathos urges them in our direction.
"Wait a moment," it says, "perhaps a compromise
could be reached, who knows?" But we are in the departure
mode. All along the autumn, the hunters'
red coats star the rubbery and decaying foliage:

"It looks as though it's been through a lot."
So that when we say we *are* sorry, that was just
a little growing accomplished too fast, no one hears us.
The time for trumpets is here, has just passed. Gosh,
and I was getting up to answer the door, and by the time

I got there no one was there. Oh, well,
there's no use crying over spilled peanuts.
But I want the one I love to be aware
that we are all cowards, not just me, and just so
we have our normal victory in the time that ordinary

arriving brought, and rooting about
enthusiastically in search of cohorts;
and when none are definitively there, why, it has grown cooler
and we can talk this over endlessly, under the vine,
quaff the abstract moonlight.

REVISIONIST HORN CONCERTO

What more clouds are there to say
how it all matters to us? Buttons, strings, bits of fluff:
it's all there, the vocabulary of displaced images,
so that if its message doesn't add up to much, whose
fault is it? I can imagine casting the answer correctly
but it doesn't work, there's no question implied
in those gorgeous, plaited ravellings. Only a little
is known about them, and nothing about their hometowns,
backgrounds, etc. Really nothing more than a masterful
way of dealing with silence, of leaving it there, and then
being off on some expedition. So nothing
works. But there is nothing there that can harm us.

Don't be afraid to let it hurt you, dance it
under morning's wire, ponder anew the shuffle between the infinite
time bomb of the Nile and today's shoelaces. Besides, these periods
have a way of elapsing, and the so-called healing process.
Does anybody care, anymore, where it went? Or whose sleep
it interrupted with a unique dissonance
of its own devising? They were always photographing
the cash register, some men came in and said it should be this way.
From now on you're in the proverbial fix. Yet what was promised
was equal to what was subtracted, while periods of socializing
in the yard made up for how the money was spent. It wasn't until
years later that someone got around to noticing the bald,
comic error that had been hidden there in the first place
to equate it with life's beginning. By then it was in full sail,
swinging on the gate of how much longer we
have to lean out of the railroad car, swaying, singing.
The foul mouth should be caked with mud and weeds by now.
But we're not going to let a little thing like that
spoil this surprise birthday, are we?
In addition to which the pole

still turns, in dreams, like the enormous wheel
of a rickshaw, viewed from up close, now
dipping into the mud and chaos, now rising like a sigh, a lark
on the mend, to remind us that all is well, or should be,
or will be shortly, given the interest in its shadow.

THE WOMAN THE LION WAS SUPPOSED TO DEFEND

And sometimes when you want it to it won't:
the space around a yodel grows deafening,
then vomits into the orchestra pit.

Yet all of this was waiting for me,
to hug me into accepting what I thought
I was losing, barrel of light down the stairs.

You know when we leave home for a short time
we can never be sure what that place will be
when we get back—some yellow tenant gibbering

in place, or, more likely the furniture
will be a shade blacker. And of course it's
up to you to find out—it's *your* problem.

Which is why I so precisely intuit
the edge of all you gave to hold back:
precisely the forlorn edge of the road

that slices through much of time and ourselves.
Don't butter it—the trees
will be officious; the frog on his own time,

a bored meter-reader. And if we can't get off the bus
why then we'll adore that patch of leopard-gray
where the schoolchildren would have assembled.

And if I had gotten laid—or mislaid—
somewhere in the cosmos, there was always an ancient
truth to speak about it. How quietly everything

conducts to this day past, urges, without pressing,
nature's monuments on us, and before you know it
we have dreamed the spectrum again. Some days

are for washing ("*this* is the way we wash our clothes"),
others for sneaking about, eating. The patchwork girl
was heard singing in her studio. For a few weeks

after I got off I was like one possessed—couldn't
find the proper forms. The silence was terrible.
But after being battered by weather and coasts,

something creamy slips in, a wedge
more or less of the temper that compounded you,
drafted you, waited for you to fall, oversaw.

The sledge of ice melts in spring sun—
more water to weep over. Soon the first picnics . . .
But they led to the black cove

pirates used to drown each other in. What was
contracted for is now scaffolding, steeped in blue.
We have ways to keep in touch with you.

HARBOR ACTIVITIES

The prospect: roofs and more roofs.
Look for a street-guide too:
anything that will attract a name.

But it doesn't mean that the getting-together
of the newborn
casts the *Lumpen* in a definitive shape
like a rafter. The clots,
cloth slits, upended
breezes could be imagined by no human wizard.
The stalls they take down argue
impenetrably. That's good. In a month's time
when the bicycle's eye scrutinizes
this landscape, we'll be vapid and know how.
Every hand has a player;
every player a new hand.

Casting for consciousness like an angler,
you make them stop to admire you.
What greater form, better force, than this?

This spreading out over the page
of someone's newspaper at breakfast?
A small thing nevertheless,

for piano left-hand,
for piano four-hands.
Later, we take the train.

IT MUST BE SOPHISTICATED

There are attics in old houses
where doubt lingers as to the corrosive
effect of night-blindness: namely,
are its victims directly linkable to a chain
of events happening elsewhere? If so,
we should shrug off resemblances

to our line of work. What was said around
the house had undue influence on one of several
shapely witnesses. And, as dames do,
she started talking to any and every
interlocutor out of harm's way. One day
you wake up and they've skipped. Or was it

always empty like this? It's hard
to remember a time when it wasn't. Maybe
your memory's playing tricks on you? Maybe
there never was such a person as Lisa Martins?
Maybe it's all over when you stand up
to walk the last mile in Enna Jettick shoes,

and they draw the blind quickly to forget you.
Once forgotten you're as good as dead,
anyway. And who would help you now?
You might as well be trapped at the bottom of a well
in the Sahara. They don't know you're alive,
or that your life was anything but exemplary

when it came time for you to live.
The fashionable present keeps queening it
over the slightly dishonorable past. Your
bridesmaids are scattered on the wind.

You don't feel like having lunch. Maybe
a walk, and a cup of tea later?

We'll see you at the end of the month!
they cried. Now it keeps ticking,
there must be a mystery down there,
darn it. I'll find it if it takes all night
and then some other sleuth can solve it.
I was only hired as a go-between. My tour is ended,

and if I've a piece of advice for you, it's
check out the rafters, the mouldings.
You can't tell who might have bargained
for clemency in your absence, leaving you holding
the bag when you got back, restless,
ready to start school, but the vagrant air's black,

what with the negative promise of spring.
The boys are still rehearsing their parts
they haven't been over, and really
it's none of my business. Said the table to the chair.
I was confined here. That's all I know,
truthfully. During the amnesty I walked

out through the open gate. The streets were full of people,
running back and forth, talking disjointedly. I was
supposed to be somewhere else, but no one knew it.
In the confusion I returned home.
Now the newshounds pester us daily.
What was I born for? More experiments?

Why are they fighting over a fuse? It doesn't
seem to be harmless like those people are listening to over there;
at the same time, everyone's a suspect in the new
climate and country. The wind turns a page

of the old tome, then another and another; soon
it's riffling through them too fast to stop.

There's nothing in it anyway. Time to move on
to another frontier beyond the transparent frieze
of foliage, guns, barges, to where he began.
Sure, dem days is gone forever, but it's the attention span
that's really gone. Back when they'd send for you
once they got a house built, it was clever

to hedge your bets and produce a fraternal twin
made of bedclothes with a mop for a wig
while you scaled the wall on a rope ladder
to be the next new thing that thinks
and cautions others not to. Far from the
inner city of conflicting attitudes, one fled with one's

holy illusions intact, one's misconceptions too, until the whole
mindset took on a largely symbolic
look, an indifferent jewel, toy
of the weather, of successive washes of light.
I can hardly believe I'm here
in this tiny republic carved out of several conflicting

principalities. It's enough, perhaps, that I was questioned
at the edge of my performance. That now I'm safe
from my own sang-froid and scores of others,
that mere forgetfulness can save up to fifty-three lives,
that they can share your power and go on glancing
upward. Because after all we were the three

original ones, the president, vice-president and treasurer
of our class. And were formed to repay
what obscure debt and be summarily
taken out of school and handed over to our parents.

It's what matters then, and after. No one
says you have to live up to principles; indeed, what are they?

What difference does it make which one came too close
in the richly darkened theater, if all
they were after was to coax you into the light,
watch you blink a minute, and then pass on, they too,
to the larger arenas, each in the wind,
in the sand, the reeds, growing? Because even if it doesn't

punish you exactly, the thing has been
lived through, the experience sealed.
O what book shall I read
now? for they are all of them new, and used,
when I write my name on the flyleaf. Look,
here is another one unread, not written. Time for you to choose.

ALBORADA

My friend, how are you?
I write with my mouth full
of crumbs in this waning summer city
as ruby grains sink majestically
to the bottom of day and others float
up past them, into something that speaks of cloud.
Do we all know we're aspected—
frightened, rather, while what comes as a ghost
continues as street life, pausing
to hitch a stocking, rambunctious, reproved,
all over the partings?
O if it were the thickness of a book,
laminated, or worse, into the meaning of chapters
that overlay one another like a horse's blankets.
But what shoots up, will.

Another day he likened it to the roar
of Paris traffic, how expensive it all seemed at first;
later, a sparrow. Besides they all get out of their cars,
stoop, and notice. Then the first one's
risen, in men's eyes. Her bathing suit
took first prize but I have to say climate never
nourished luck more, nor came out as an extraordinary
pencilled thing draped across rooftops
for all to see, till they saw, and the resultant gold-rush
landed us in the pokey. Here, as ever, some
are believers. Top-notch achievers.
In this way one gets to do it
and become one's self. Never
again did the small matter of a raised
skylight's hasp sicken the winter, the kitten.

By evening only the thought rained.

HOW TO CONTINUE

Oh there once was a woman
and she kept a shop
selling trinkets to tourists
not far from a dock
who came to see what life could be
far back on the island.

And it was always a party there
always different but very nice
New friends to give you advice
or fall in love with you which is nice
and each grew so perfectly from the other
it was a marvel of poetry
and irony

And in this unsafe quarter
much was scary and dirty
but no one seemed to mind
very much
the parties went on from house to house
There were friends and lovers galore
all around the store
There was moonshine in winter
and starshine in summer
and everybody was happy to have discovered
what they discovered

And then one day the ship sailed away
There were no more dreamers just sleepers
in heavy attitudes on the dock
moving as if they knew how
among the trinkets and the souvenirs
the random shops of modern furniture

and a gale came and said
it is time to take all of you away
from the tops of the trees to the little houses
on little paths so startled

And when it became time to go
they none of them would leave without the other
for they said we are all one here
and if one of us goes the other will not go
and the wind whispered it to the stars
the people all got up to go
and looked back on love

Permissions Acknowledgments

Grateful acknowledgment is hereby made to the publications in which many
of the poems in this book first appeared:
A Garland for Stephen Spender, "Seasonal"; *American Poetry Review*, "Double
Sestina"; *Antaeus*, "Just Wednesday"; *Bad Henry Review*, "In Vain, Therefore";
Black Warrior Review, "The Art of Speeding"; *Boulevard*, "That You Tell";
Bridge Book, [untitled]; *Broadway 2*, "A Mourning Forbidding Valediction";
The Bulletin, "Susan," "The Old Complex"; *Conjunctions*, "Autumn on the
Thruway," "It Must Be Sophisticated"; *Cuz*, "The King"; *Denver Quarterly*,
"Avant de Quitter Ces Lieux"; *Gold Coast*, "Autumn Telegram"; *Grand Street*,
"Of Dreams and Dreaming," "The Beer Drinkers"; *Harvard Advocate*, "A
Hole in Your Sock"; *Harvard Book Review*, "Another Example"; *Hodos*, "From
Palookaville"; *Joe Soap's Canoe*, "The Whole Is Admirably Composed";
Michigan Quarterly Review, "Irresolutions on a Theme of La Rochefoucauld";
Mudfish, "The White Shirt"; *New American Writing*, *"Oeuvres Complètes"*;
The New Yorker, "Baked Alaska," "Brute Image," "Film Noir," "Hotel
Lautréamont," "In Another Time," "Love's Old Sweet Song," "Notes from
the Air," "The Phantom Agents," "Poem at the New Year," "Still Life with
Stranger," "The Garden of False Civility," "The Large Studio," "Withered
Compliments"; *The New York Review of Books*, "A Sedentary Existence,"
"As Oft It Chanceth," "Erebus," "From Estuaries, from Casinos," "On the
Empress's Mind"; *o-blek*, "Villanelle," "Wild Boys of the Road"; *Occident*,
"Kamarinskaya"; *Painted Bride Quarterly*, "The Great Bridge Game of Life";

The Paris Review, "Korean Soap Opera," "Musica Reservata," "Of Linnets and Dull Time," "The Departed Lustre," "The Youth's Magic Horn"; *PN Review,* "Alborada," "American Bar," "And Socializing," "Elephant Visitors," "From Palookaville," "How to Continue," "In My Way/On My Way," *"Le Mensonge de Nina Petrovna,"* "Not Now but in Forty-five Minutes"; *Poetry New York,* "The Little Black Dress"; *Poetry Review, "Avant de Quitter Ces Lieux"; Private,* "A Stifled Notation"; *Scripsi,* "Where We Went for Lunch"; *Shiny,* "Quartet"; *Soho Square,* "Livelong Days"; *Southwest Review,* "Livelong Days"; *Times Literary Supplement,* "A Driftwood Altar," "And Forgetting," "Autumn Telegram," "Joy," "Light Turnouts," "Part of the Superstition," "Private Syntax," "Retablo," "Revisionist Horn Concerto"; *Voices,* "Central Air," "Harbor Activities"; *The World,* "The Wind Talking"; *Yale Review,* "A Call for Papers."

A Note About the Author

John Ashbery is the author of fourteen previous books of poetry, including *April Galleons* (1987), and of a volume of art criticism, *Reported Sightings* (1989). His *Self-Portrait in a Convex Mirror* received the Pulitzer Prize for poetry, as well as the National Book Critics Circle Award and the National Book Award. He has been named a Guggenheim Fellow and a MacArthur Fellow, and is a chancellor of the Academy of American Poets. In 1989–90 he was Charles Eliot Norton Professor of Poetry at Harvard. In 1992 he was awarded the Ruth Lilly Poetry Prize and the Antonio Feltrinelli International Prize for Poetry. He is currently Charles P. Stevenson, Jr. Professor of Languages and Literature at Bard College.

A Note on the Type

This book was set in a digitized version of Granjon, a type named in compliment to Robert Granjon, a type cutter and printer active, in Antwerp, Lyons, Rome, and Paris, from 1523 to 1590. Granjon, the boldest and most original designer of his time, was one of the first to practice the trade of type founder apart from that of printer.

Linotype Granjon was designed by George W. Jones, who based his drawings on a face used by Claude Garamond (c. 1480–1561) in his beautiful French books. Granjon more closely resembles Garamond's own type than does any of the various modern faces that bear his name.

Composed by Brevis Press, Bethany, Connecticut
Printed and bound by Halliday Lithographers,
West Hanover, Massachusetts
Designed by Iris Weinstein

21 397 101

9/96

NOV 2 2 1998